MW01281873

THE HEALING POWER OF PRAYING THE ROSARY

LOYOLA PRESS.
A JESUIT MINISTRY

LOYOLA PRESS.
A JESUIT MINISTRY

www.loyolapress.com

Cover art credit: Tinyevilhog/Moment/Getty Images

ISBN: 978-0-8294-5900-5
Library of Congress Control Number: 2024947784

Published in Chicago, IL
Printed in the United States of America.
24 25 26 27 28 29 30 31 32 33 Versa 10 9 8 7 6 5 4 3 2 1

*Meditation engages thought, imagination, emotion,
and desire. This mobilization of faculties is necessary in
order to deepen our convictions of faith, prompt
the conversion of our heart, and strengthen our will
to follow Christ. Christian prayer tries above all to meditate
on the mysteries of Christ, as in Lectio divina or the rosary.
This form of prayerful reflection is of great value,
but Christian prayer should go further: to the knowledge
of the love of the Lord Jesus, to union with him.*

—Catechism of the Catholic Church

For my mom, Roseanne Jansen.

The ghosts of those I love
haunt me in the sorrowful stillness,
not leering, capricious ghosts,
but loving ghosts
who touch my brow with tender care.
—Jack Kerouac

CONTENTS

BACKSTORY

Twenty years ago, I wrote a short book on the Rosary, my very first book, now long out of print, in which I shared the following story:

I had been working out at a local gym. One evening, a jacked trainer with arms the size of small countries approached me as I finished a set of exercises and said, "You're carrying too much weight."

"Excuse me?" I replied.

"Too much weight," he repeated. "You're doing the exercise wrong. You're going to hurt yourself."

I stared at him for a moment as my ego processed what he was saying. The trainer pulled the pin out of the machine, reduced the weight by more than half, and showed me the proper form for the exercise.

"You try it," he said.

I did. I could barely lift the lighter weight.

Walking home that evening, the trainer's words kept running through my head, reminding me of a Beatles song, "Carry That Weight." Later that night, as I prayed the Rosary, which had recently become my before-sleep ritual, and meditated on the Sorrowful Mysteries of Christ, it hit me.

You're carrying too much weight.

Words from the Bible I hadn't thought of in some time flooded my mind: "Come to me, all you that are weary and are carrying heavy burdens, and I will give you rest" (Matthew 11:28).

I asked myself then (and I ask myself now), *Why had life become so burdensome?* At that time, I was running on a spiritual high. I had returned to the faith of my youth, I was praying every day, and I experienced levels of peace that felt unimaginable for someone who grew up in a family that epitomized the word dysfunction. My career was progressing, my young family was happy, and I was living my dream as a writer and editor. And then that spiritual high just crashed. God seemed to have gone on vacation, leaving me alone in the dog days of summer. I didn't mind the heat so much as the tedium of monotonously repetitive, lazy days; a long drought of the soul ensued. Like arid ground that becomes cracked and desiccated beneath a relentless sun, I felt broken, dry, and depleted.

Still, like a good farmer back in the nineteenth century, and with rosary in hand, I would pray for rain.

The rain never came. Some tumbleweed, yes, and dry lightning, and an occasional drop of water on my head when clouds teased the possibility of relief (come to think of it, those drops might not have been rain).

That night after the gym encounter, as I prayed the Rosary (with a special intention for my mom), I realized that maybe God wasn't the problem. Maybe the problem was me. Maybe

I wasn't listening to God. I came to the revelation that the Rosary isn't a way of getting God's attention; the Rosary is a way of getting *me* to *pay attention*.

That moment of revelation was a moment of grace. With that newfound awareness, I allowed myself to be healed by the presence of Jesus. This healing was not just emotional or mental. It was also deeply spiritual—a restoration of my soul's balance in relation to life's burdens. The Rosary, with its rhythmic prayers, became a channel for me to find holistic healing by connecting my mind, and body, and spirit, each part to the other. My life was never again the same. The desert of spiritual dryness gave way to a renewal of spirit, with the Rosary the oasis creating a cool island of lush vegetation. What's my point? Simply, the Rosary can change your life by opening your eyes to seeing God, and opening your ears to hearing God.

This is a book about learning to pray to Jesus with Mary through the Rosary, which is both a devotion in honor of Mary and also a unique way of getting to know her Son. It's true that there are many wonderful, poetic, practical, insightful books that have been written on the Rosary, and I will mention a few in the pages that follow. But this book, which is centered on the Rosary as a meditative experience, is different. This book includes a mini-exploration of some of the neuroscience behind the benefits we receive through spiritual practices like praying the Rosary.

We live in times of personal, national, and global anxiety. Times when more and more people are turning away from organized religion. One of the reasons for this rejection is a lack of "evidence" for God: Why believe in something when there is (seemingly) no evidence for its existence? This book doesn't look to prove anything to anyone, and it certainly doesn't look to science to prove that God is real. But what it does do is offer evidence about how a devotion like the Rosary can heal us spiritually *and* physically. Since our bodies and souls are integral to our existence, how we treat the soul affects the body, and how we treat the body affects the soul. Hurt one and you hurt the other. Heal one, and you heal the other.

Many of us attempt to do too much in our lives. We're like busy Martha in the Bible, who needed the example of her sister, Mary, sitting at the feet of Jesus, listening to his teachings to understand what is most essential in our lives. Jesus kindly explained to Martha that her sister had her priorities straight.

The Rosary allows us to get our priorities straight.

This is not a long book. As a writer, I believe in the get-in-and-get-out method, and I live by the philosophy of never staying too long at a party. What follows are a series of reflections, insights, and practical techniques for praying the Rosary so that you might elevate your spiritual practice.

It is my prayer that this little book takes some of the weight—the "too much weight"—from your shoulders. And eases some of the pressure you're feeling. And maybe even helps to heal wherever it is that you feel worn down or broken. My hope is that you see this beautiful devotion in a new light so that, like me, you too can spend time with Jesus, sit in his presence, and be open to the healing power of his love.

FULL OF GRACE

The Rosary has had a life-altering, healing impact on my life. This book explores the origins of that impact and how you can benefit from making this simple devotion that has been cherished by the faithful, the troubled, the inquisitive, and the weary for more than nine centuries a part of your daily life.

Often viewed as a distinctly Catholic practice focusing on the birth, life, death, and resurrection of Jesus, the Rosary is a universal prayer that offers new levels of awareness of Christ by deepening our sensitivity to Jesus, which in turn brings about a richer understanding of ourselves. Through this growing awareness, we broaden our ability to live our lives anchored in love.

Or, as my grandmother Nana used to say, "When we get to know Jesus, we get to know why Jesus loves us so much."

I loved my Nana and heeded the blue-collar wisdom she shared with me as I was growing up. That being said, for much of my life I didn't think Jesus liked me, let alone loved me. There are many reasons why I thought this, some of which I've covered in previous books, including *Holy Ghosts* and *Station to Station*.[1] The point here is that I endured seemingly endless dark nights of the soul.

Case in point: In the Backstory of this book, I mentioned that on the night of the gym-inspired insight, I prayed the Rosary with the intention of my mother in mind. At that time, my mom had found herself in a rather precarious situation. Financial constraints and the complexities of the ordeal made the problems seem insurmountable. Her mental health and her very future were on the line, and I tried to help her as best I could.

At the same time, my wife and I were new parents, and my involvement in the dealings to extract my mom from her difficulties carried a weight so great that it threatened my marriage. I felt as if I were stuck between Scylla and Charybdis, with either option untenable, if not disastrous. I felt as if I had no firm footing. As if I were treading water. And that consoling presence? It was nowhere to be found.

I remember sitting in my mom's living room sometime after the gym incident feeling overwhelmed with anxiety. I was worried about my mom, myself, my wife, and our child. Then, as if something *within* me was praying *through* me, I began praying the Hail Mary. Over and over, I prayed the Hail Mary. My thought, and, I suppose, my hope, was that maybe another mom could help us out here. Without consciously realizing I was doing it, my mind slipped easily into a practice I had learned as a kid in Catholic school. The practice of praying the Rosary.

That day, as I murmured, "Hail Mary, full of grace, the Lord is with thee," I prayed for a miracle. And do you know what happened?

Nothing. Not a darn thing.

There was no miraculous solution, no sudden resolution to our problems, not even a flash of insight as to how I could help my mom.

And yet . . .

And yet a sense of calm washed over me.

It reminded me of a time when I was a teenager, swimming at the beach on a particularly windy day. I had swum farther out than I should have; eventually, I started to panic that I wasn't going to make it back. I began swimming parallel to the shore, trying to inch my way back to land, quickly growing ever more tired and frightened. Then a large wave came crashing over me. It thrust me down under the water, which was terrifying. But it also it moved me forward. When I surfaced, my feet were able to make contact with the sandy shore, and I realized that I was safe.

Immersing myself spontaneously in this prayer engendered a similar sense of safety. Peace. The welcome sensation of solid ground beneath my feet.

Had I been rescued? I don't know, but that feeling of calm enabled me to banish the fear response, which in turn opened up my rational mind, and I was able to help my mom navigate her challenges with dignity and optimism. The struggles remained, but the burdens felt lighter. Something happened. Something full of grace. Mary wrapped her arms around me and took me to a place of love.

Since that fateful day, the Rosary has become part of the very fabric of my being.

And I've come to see that healing through prayer is not always instantaneous or miraculous but, like many things, it is a process. Each time I pray, I feel another part of my wounded spirit, mind, or body being touched by divine grace. Just as a physical wound takes time to heal, so, too, do the hurts of our hearts and souls.

The Rosary is a prayer of devotion, of reverence. And like all prayer it is the gateway to a communion with Jesus. It is a meditative practice in which we focus on a unique aspect of the sacred, a practice that can transform our lives by attuning us to God's voice. Devotion quiets the chatter so that we can hear and experience the divine in a deeply personal way. Of all the Catholic devotions, the Rosary is by far the one that can draw us to an elevated experience of Christ, by the sheer fact that it requires about fifteen to twenty minutes to pray, which is just enough time to enter into a contemplative state without necessarily feeling fatigued and falling asleep.

The Rosary is a Marian prayer, meaning it is a prayer of Mary, but most important it is a way for Mary to bring forth an experience of her Son. The mysteries and stories within the Rosary focus on Jesus. While Christ is at the center of the Rosary, it is Mary who guides us there. She brings us closer to God by amplifying his still, small voice in ways we can experience and comprehend, offering a uniquely human perspective in celebrating the life of Jesus. This is one of the glories of the Rosary.

In the Magnificat, Mary's song of praise upon learning she would be the mother of Jesus, Mary says that her soul magnifies the Lord. She does just that in the Rosary. By drawing closer to Mary—Jesus's mother, our mother—we find that God's presence in our lives is magnified through our senses in sight, sound, touch, motion, and even smell. In other words, as we come to know Jesus better through our sensory experiences, we get better at knowing God in all things.

One of the best ways of engaging our senses in spiritual practice is through our imagination, which elevates our sensory experiences to something beyond the known world. Something that touches the soul. As we shall see in the pages to follow, one of the most effective ways to elevate the spiritual life is by engaging the imagination in praying the Rosary.

IMAGINE

Imagine that you've fallen deeply in love with the person of your dreams. Visualize this ideal partner—stunning to look at, intelligent, wise, loving, loyal, and a friend unlike any other. In their presence, you feel special. You are energized, inspired, amazed. You feel as if you are limitless.

This love surpasses any you've known. It's mutual and it's nurturing, and it makes you more utterly human. Perhaps your soul, long dormant, has been awakened by this person. You sense a transformation within yourself. The world, once obscured by diaphanous veils, brightens with every step you take toward your beloved. Colors intensify, sounds sharpen, and everyday noises morph into music. For the first time since childhood, you experience wonder.

As your relationship deepens, time seems to revolve around just the two of you—until the day your beloved invites you to meet their parents. Anxiety grips you. What will they think of you? Are you worthy? Though you've managed to keep some flaws from your beloved, parents, especially mothers, have a way of seeing through facades.

Despite your nerves, your beloved reassures you. On the day of the meeting, as you approach their parents' home, the

7

hand of your beloved tucked inside your sweaty palm steadies your nerves. You feel intimidated because your beloved is complete; by comparison, you feel less than whole. The door opens, and you meet Mom. She is beauty and kindness personified as she warmly welcomes you into the family. All your fears dissolve in her presence.

You look around. Although you don't see the father, you sense his presence everywhere.

Now, let's take a step back. You've never experienced a love like this, and while you feel open, your beloved remains a mystery. You have questions. It's not that you don't feel close, but you crave knowing absolutely everything about your beloved. You wonder, *What were you like as a child? What were your parents doing before they had you? What were your friends like? Did you ever get lost? Were you ever lonely? Frightened? And why did you come into my life?*

You've held off asking these questions of your beloved, but, strangely, in front of Mom, you feel comfortable enough to pose them. To find out more. She seems ready to embrace you by helping you understand everything. Who better to provide insight than the woman who carried your beloved for nine months?

You start asking your questions. She smiles and takes a scrapbook from a shelf, and you begin looking at pictures together. "This is me when I first found out I was going to have a baby," she says. "Here's one after I gave birth. So many people came to visit us. Here are pictures from a wedding we attended."

You sit with her, paging through this treasure chest of memories. The pictures tell stories, revealing the happiness, sorrows, and joys of her family. Your worries, fears, and doubts melt away, and by the grace of God you are transformed by love.

Just as Mary's motherly presence calms us in our fears, the Rosary itself can become a tool for healing our anxieties. This reparative influence happens as we get to know Jesus better. And Mary is the key to understanding Christ in our lives. It begins with the Annunciation, when she learns of God's incarnation within her. Thus, the Christ story begins with the announcement that God is within each of us. Just as Mary carried Jesus, we are called to permit Jesus to grow in us, to carry Jesus within us every moment of the day. This spiritual gestation takes place over a lifetime. The more we nurture God within us, the more we become vessels of the divine for others; the more we care for this inner Christ child, the more we give life to the presence that gives life to us.

Nice words, but how do we accomplish this calling?

One way is to *do what Jesus did*. The Gospels, among other things, are the acts of Jesus, a prequel to the Acts of the Apostles, which is the adventures of Christ's followers. The Gospels show us Christ in action—Christ preaching, listening, educating, healing. The Gospels also show us how

Jesus dealt with suffering. Nothing in Scripture or tradition ever said there would be no suffering. Each generation beats their breasts and wails, *Why does God allow suffering?* but there is no simple answer that satisfies. Suffering exists. Predictably, Jesus showed us through his Passion how to act when life and the world seem to be closing in on us.

The other way is to *just be*. Be in the presence of Jesus. Focus on the present moment. Try as hard as you can not to think about the past or ruminate on the future. I love this piece of wisdom from St. Thérèse of Lisieux: "If I did not simply live from one moment to another, it would be impossible for me to be patient, but I only look at the present, I forget the past, and I take good care not to forestall the future. When we yield to discouragement or despair, it is usually because we think too much about the past and the future."[2]

In other words, be here now.

When we cultivate ways of being in God's presence through prayer and meditation, we enter a space where these spiritual practices may not even be necessary. Like Martha in the Bible, we do a lot—we take care of our families, we go to work or school, we feed our families and houseguests—but, as we talked about earlier, Martha's sister, Mary, demonstrates the better way to spend our time. As James notes in his letter in the New Testament, right action is good. But sometimes we just need to sit at Jesus's feet and do nothing. Sometimes we just need to spend time with him and chill. When we do, we lay claim to a special grace, a form of spiritual osmosis where we absorb something of our Creator in a way that energizes and heals.

In my book *Station to Station*, I offer a new way of seeing the Stations of the Cross as a series of responses to difficulties in our lives rather than strictly as a journey of suffering. Of course, the Stations, which is literally a chronicle of Jesus walking to his death, is a journey in much the same way that the Rosary is a journey. To pray the Rosary is to walk through the life and times of Jesus and his mother. Over the years, however, the Rosary has become for me less a journey, more a way of spending time with family.

For some time now, I have referred to Jesus as my brother from another mother. This is meant as a term of endearment, a way of expressing closeness for a friend you hold dear. But I could also say that Jesus is a brother from my mother or, even better, *our* mother. As the mother of Jesus, Mary is our mother too, and as the mother of the universal Church she shares a special bond with us. She is someone who watches over us, someone who acts on our behalf. And we share with Mary the indwelling of Christ. Just as Mary carried Jesus physically, we also carry Jesus—spiritually—within us.

This makes us arks of the covenant. You may recall from the Bible that the ark was the case in which was enclosed the Word of God in the form of the Ten Commandments. We carry the Word within us, too; we carry within us Christ, "the Word," as described by John in his Gospel. And just as Mary loved and cared for the baby she carried within, so, too, are we called to love and care for Christ by keeping his commandments.

This is to say that we are all family—at a spiritual level and at a physical level too. (Although this is not a book about our shared DNA, humanity does share a cellular history that goes all the way back to the Big Bang, and probably even before that moment.) By seeing Mary as our mother and Jesus as our brother, we open ourselves to the intimacy that can be found in familial relationships. This intimacy is crucial for discovering our true identity as children of God. As Pope Benedict XVI said, "The family is fundamental because that is where the first awareness of the meaning of life germinates in the human soul."[3] Through this formation, we increasingly become who we are meant to be.

Granted, family can be a double-edged sword. Few of us come from a family that has no issues; we come equipped with our own personal quirks, idiosyncrasies, traumas, and baggage. Nevertheless, many of us choose to put up with dysfunction and spend time together. When things are going right—no bickering, no fighting, no hurt feelings, no jealousies—families can exist as powerful manifestations of love and care.

The good news: while we might bring our own pain and sorrow to the mix when we engage with the Rosary, Mary and Jesus seem to have worked out all their issues, which means we have a family we can always turn to for advice, support, and healing. We do that through praying the Rosary.

Though Jesus is God, Jesus was also human, born of a human mother, and together they shared the highs and weathered the lows of life. The Rosary shares in those highs and lows, as if to reassure us, "I understand what you are going through. I'm here to help if you have questions or you need me. Or I can simply sit here beside you and just listen."

THE ROSARY

The word "rosary" comes from the Latin *rosarium*, meaning "a garden or garland of roses." This is a fitting origin for a prayer of such beauty. The Rosary is a centuries-old form of meditation; it has been a prayer tradition using beads since before the Reformation. Popularized in the thirteenth century by St. Dominic and the Dominican Order of Preachers, the repetition of prayers effectively combines meditation with devotion.

The basic structure of the Rosary involves a sequence of prayers that is composed of four sets of Gospel mysteries. These four sets are Joyful, Sorrowful, Luminous, and Glorious. Each set features five significant events in Christ's life. Each event is a decade, which is a prayer (traditionally the Hail Mary) repeated ten times. Other prayers, notably the Our Father and the Glory Be, are interspersed throughout the Rosary. Throughout the cycle of prayers, Mary keeps the focus on Jesus as she guides us through her Son's life.

Though all four sets can be prayed in one sitting, the more usual practice is to focus on one set at a time. Initially, repeating the same prayers may seem challenging, but practice reveals the value of repetition. Life's greatest gifts are repetitious: our heartbeats, our breathing, the cyclical movements of nights, days, seasons, and the circle of life.

A common misconception, alluded to earlier, is that the Rosary is a prayer to Mary. It's not. A better understanding of the Rosary is that it is a way of praying *with* Mary. Suppose you're talking with a friend who asks for your prayers during tough times. Praying the Rosary is like that. It's a spiritual union, an act of generosity, selflessness, and love. Pope John Paul II described the Rosary as a prayer of learning and illumination that brings us into communion with Jesus through Mary's heart.[4]

UNDERSTANDING THE MYSTERIES OF THE ROSARY

Mystery can leave us feeling unsettled, puzzled, and perplexed. In suspense movies and novels, typically the main character must confront a bewildering situation—something has happened, but why, and who is responsible? The protagonist then spends the rest of the story uncovering the answers.

If the best mysteries have twists and turns that push our intellectual limits by keeping us guessing, then the stories that make up the Rosary are the greatest mysteries of all time. They are filled with colorful characters, inexplicable events, and twists and turns in plotlines, all of which beckon our attention and involvement. But unlike an ordinary detective novel, the Rosary asks you to check your intellect at the door. These are scenes of faith. While it's important to ask questions like *Why did this happen?*, *How did this happen?*, and *Who's responsible?*, this prayer asks something different of us. These meditative investigations are best experienced not through rational, logical thinking but rather in *feeling* the mysteries with your heart.

Allow me to explain. Conceive an image in your mind of a friend who has just received bad news. This person is emotional and upset. You could talk to your friend about what happened, offering your opinions and advice. Or you could sit quietly with your friend, listening and genuinely empathizing. Although you are keenly aware of your friend and his pain and everything going on around you, you're not interfering by talking or by allowing your own thoughts to roam. You are simply there, fully present and committed to experiencing the moment. Your focused presence speaks louder than words.

Or imagine being with a couple who has just had a baby. Of course words of joy and excitement and congratulations are exchanged, but at some point everyone falls silent and simply gazes with awe upon the new life that has come into the world. In your awareness of the ineffable mystery of life, you are experiencing something significant. You are moving from the mind, a place of thought and opinion, to the heart, a place of feeling and experience.

The Rosary originally contained three sets of mysteries: the Joyful, the Sorrowful, and the Glorious, each corresponding to a different period in the life of Jesus Christ and his mother. These mysteries cover Jesus's early years, his Passion, and his Resurrection. In 2002, Pope John Paul II added a fourth set of mysteries. Known as the Luminous Mysteries (also known as the Mysteries of Light), this set of mysteries focuses on the redemptive power of Christ's ministry.

The Rosary is composed of the following four sets of mysteries and the five events contained within each:

Joyful

The Annunciation

The Visitation

The Nativity of Jesus

The Presentation of
    the Infant Jesus
    in the Temple

The Finding of Jesus
    in the Temple

Luminous

The Baptism of Jesus
    in the River Jordan

The Manifestation
    at Cana

The Proclamation of the
    Kingdom of God

The Transfiguration
    of Jesus

The Last Supper

Sorrowful

The Agony in the Garden

The Scourging of Jesus
    at the Pillar

The Crowning of Jesus
    with Thorns

The Carrying of the Cross
    by Jesus

The Crucifixion of Jesus

Glorious

The Resurrection

The Ascension of Jesus
    to Heaven

The Descent of the
    Holy Spirit upon
    the Apostles

The Assumption of Mary

The Crowning of Mary as
    the Queen of Heaven

THE JOYFUL MYSTERIES

The Joyful Mysteries focus on the miracle of the Incarnation, when the divine and the human unite in Jesus Christ. The Annunciation begins with the angel Gabriel appearing to Mary, telling her she will be the mother of the Messiah. Next is the Visitation, when Mary visits her older cousin Elizabeth, who is also pregnant. Elizabeth's son, John, will become John the Baptist, who prepares the way for Jesus. The Nativity follows, celebrating the birth of Jesus and the arrival of shepherds and wise men who honor the newborn King. Eight days later, Jesus is presented at the temple, where Mary and Joseph meet Simeon, a man filled with the Holy Spirit. The Joyful Mysteries conclude with the story of Mary and Joseph finding the young Jesus preaching to scholars and holy people in the temple.

THE LUMINOUS MYSTERIES

The Luminous Mysteries begin with John baptizing Jesus in the river Jordan, and the Holy Spirit descends upon Jesus, marking the start of Jesus's ministry. The next mystery is the wedding at Cana, when Jesus performs his first public miracle at Mary's request. Then comes Jesus's proclamation of the Kingdom of God, in which Jesus emphasizes that the Kingdom is present in the here and now. The Transfiguration, when Jesus is revealed in his divine glory alongside Moses and

Elijah, follows. The Luminous Mysteries conclude with the Last Supper, when, in sharing his final meal with his disciples, Jesus offers the bread and wine of eternal life.

THE SORROWFUL MYSTERIES

The Sorrowful Mysteries focus on the Passion of Christ. They begin with the Agony in the Garden, when Jesus prays for strength to accept his suffering. The Scourging at the Pillar follows, depicting Jesus being brutally beaten by Roman authorities. Next is the Crowning with Thorns, when Jesus is mocked and crowned with a painful wreath of thorns. The Carrying of the Cross shows Jesus bearing his cross through Jerusalem's streets. The Sorrowful Mysteries culminate in the Crucifixion, when Jesus is nailed to the cross, with his mother Mary, John, and Mary Magdalene remaining steadfast at the foot of his cross.

THE GLORIOUS MYSTERIES

The Glorious Mysteries start with the Resurrection, celebrating Jesus rising from the dead, thereby becoming our hope for eternal salvation. The Ascension follows, when Jesus blesses his disciples and is taken up to Heaven. Next is the Descent of the Holy Spirit, when Mary and the apostles receive the Holy Spirit and begin their mission to spread the Good News. The Assumption highlights when God assumes Mary's body into Heaven. The Glorious Mysteries conclude with Mary's Coronation, when she is crowned in Heaven, signifying her eternal glory and importance in the divine plan.

PRAYING WITH IMAGINATION

By reflecting on these mysteries, and with Mary's unwavering faith as our guide, we embark on a spiritual journey through the pivotal moments of Jesus Christ's life. Each mystery invites us to meditate on the profound events they encapsulate, allowing us to experience their significance. As we pray the Rosary, we are not merely reciting words; we have been invited to immerse ourselves in the divine narrative, an involvement that transforms each prayer into a moment of intimate connection with God. This meditative practice requires more than just time; it demands our presence and willingness to fully engage our hearts and minds. As we immerse ourselves in these sacred moments, we can experience healing through our deep connection with Jesus and Mary. By placing ourselves in the midst of their story, we allow their love and the grace they extend to affect us by gently repairing, restoring, rejuvenating, and reviving the woundedness we carry.

Most of us can pray the prayers of one cycle of mysteries in about fifteen minutes, even taking time to ponder the Scripture that inspired each mystery. That's literally one percent of your day, though we should by no means rush to get through the prayers, because the best effects happen when we take our time so that we can experience our soul's reaction to the stories of Christ's life. As priest and theologian Romano Guardini writes in *The Rosary of Our Lady*, "The Rosary is a prayer of lingering. One must take one's time for it, putting the necessary time at its disposal, not only externally but internally. One who wants to pray it rightly must put away those things that press upon him and become for a time purposeless and quiet."[5]

Some people think that the Rosary is boring with all the repetitive prayers. Understood. We live in a world where we are constantly overstimulated by noise and images, so slowing down and repeating the same prayer over and over again can feel, at first blush, like a chore. Or we may have become so accustomed to being immersed in sights and sounds, we may find it almost impossible to settle ourselves enough to separate from the world and sit with Mary in this way. But by using our imagination to place us alongside Christ, we can take praying the Rosary to a new level of experience. By allowing this repetitive spiritual exercise to bloom vibrantly and beautifully, we become open receptacles to a trove of spiritual riches and rewards.

The bread that is used for the Eucharist is dry and flavorless, and yet our faith tells us that within that tiny wafer is the great power and presence of Christ. The Rosary offers something similar. The time devoted to the Rosary is time set aside to experience a power and presence that brings us closer to the living God.

LEARNING TO
HEAR GOD'S VOICE

God is always speaking to us. The reason we suffer, worry, feel fear, and experience disjointedness and confusion is because we don't realize that the answers to our questions and the balm for our suffering are right in front of us—or, perhaps more accurately, right inside of us. Healing often begins when we quiet the noise around us and listen to God's gentle voice. The simple act of being still in his presence allows his healing grace to flow through us. And yet, we often don't hear. We don't hear God speaking to us. And why is that? Because most of the time we don't quiet our own noise.

Have you ever tried to listen to two conversations at once? It's nearly impossible. You get fragments of each and neither makes sense. Now, call to mind what it's like to try to listen in on two conversations while you are talking to someone else. You can't even understand the person you're talking to!

You might protest, *I'm a quiet person. I'm respectful. I don't interrupt. And I'm a good listener. So why can't I hear God?*

It's because even if we're not vocalizing, our minds are racing with ideas, questions, worries, and details, details, details. Some of the quietest people—the great introverts of the world—have the most clamorous minds.

Try the following experiment:

1. Find a watch or clock with a second hand.
2. Take a few moments to relax. Breathe deeply.
3. Try not to think about anything for ten seconds.

Did you think of something? Of course you did. It's almost impossible to halt the unceasing stream of thoughts that runs through your mind. Thinking is a perpetually ongoing state of being, and for some of us, it's a very bad habit indeed.

But, you protest (and rightly so), *if I'm constantly thinking, speaking, and doing—in other words, if I'm constantly drowning out God with my own personal white noise—how can I center myself enough to hear God's voice?*

Through prayer.

But isn't prayer about talking to God? No one ever taught me how to listen during prayer.

Again, you're not wrong. Almost everyone believes that prayer is communicating with God. And that is true. The better way to understand prayer is that it is a tool for preparing your mind, body, and soul for a state of being in which you can communicate with God in a nonverbal way. It's a way of quieting your restless heart, mind, and soul so that you can focus your whole attention on God and bask in an experience of unity without thoughts, without words, without expectations.

One of the best ways to reach this state is through repetitious prayer like the Rosary. The combination of repeating prayers and allowing space and time for meditation has the effect of calming our minds. We just need to shift our attention from *thinking* to *listening*. There's no room here for worried thoughts. In this new space, we naturally surrender to God who will feed and care for and protect us. God who loves us so much that he has given us not only his Son but also the mother of his Beloved.

WHY DO WE PRAY THE ROSARY?

The Rosary isn't the only prayer to help you hear God, but for me it's been the most effective. We go through life *not living in the moment*—a phrase that has become a cliché in self-help circles. Motivational gurus tell us that living in the moment makes us happier and more fulfilled. I subscribe to this advice because I have learned through experience that when we aren't living in the moment, we miss out on the gift of presence.

I can say this with authority because I'm a worrier. I've been a worrier all my life. I spend a lot of mental energy rewinding the past and worrying about the future. I'm almost never in the absolute here and now. But this describes pre-Rosary Gary Jansen. The Rosary helped me change all of that by helping me move closer to the present, thereby moving me closer to the Kingdom of God, which is at hand, right here, right now. Perhaps most important, the prayer refocuses my attention away from my anxieties and toward the face of Christ, where there are no words, just an experience of being present with beauty.

The Rosary is a spiritual exercise, yes, but part of its power arises from physiological experience. The structure of repetition and a focus on meditation—which is nothing more than observing a scene without attaching words to it, allowing thoughts to pass by like clouds in the sky, without judgment or analysis—have a soothing effect on the body. The combination helps to regulate breathing, reduce stress, and relax muscles. A friend of mine once berated himself for falling asleep while saying the Rosary. But why should he be upset? He should be thankful. Falling asleep in the arms of God is a precious blessing.

The more you practice the prayer, exploring how the mysteries relate to your life, the more your day-to-day worries will be eclipsed by the life of Christ. Even though you are doing several things at once—fingering a bead, saying a prayer, contemplating a mystery—your eyes and ears grow more attuned to God. You begin to wake up spiritually. There will be times of silence in between thoughts and words, and in that silence your awareness of the people and things around you will expand. You'll have more appreciation for creation. You'll feel more alive as you begin to see yourself as part of the Holy Presence you seek.

You might wonder how reciting prayers during the Rosary can qualify as "being quiet." It's because saying these prayers silences thoughts that crowd your mind. The more you pray, the more automatic each prayer becomes. The words, while important, are secondary to the prayerfully meditative experience where we aim to refocus on God. After all, Jesus made it clear that God knows our words even before they are born in our minds and expressed in our hearts.

The turning of our gaze to Christ helps us understand our true needs in life. God already knows what these needs are, but we learn from our journey what we truly need, what we truly desire.

Many people get frustrated and stop praying because they don't sense that God is listening. I've experienced this myself. It can feel like a letdown, a silly exercise that reaps no rewards. But the Rosary is like taking a multivitamin. Does anyone ever really feel better after taking a multivitamin? Most people will feel nothing (though I must admit sometimes I feel a little queasy after swallowing one). And yet, over time those vitamins and minerals have positive effects on your mind and body. We could say those ingredients fill in the gaps. So, too, does prayer.

Of course, there are the mystics and saints, who attest that we are never out of earshot of God. Our interpretations of feelings—that we are alone, or unworthy, or beyond help—may tell us otherwise. But feelings and their interpretations do not equate to truth. Feelings can change in an instant. You may feel happy one day, sad the next, confident one day, unsure the next. What has changed? Are you not the same person? Put another way, if God were to strip you of your doubts and your confidence, who would you be?

Imagine you want to talk to your friend, so you call him, but he doesn't answer. You leave a message. A few days go by and your friend hasn't returned your call. You call again and leave another message. You follow up with a couple of texts. Days pass and still no return call. Not even a thumbs-up emoji. You feel confused—*Why is my friend ignoring me?* Then you get a little miffed. *Why am I being ghosted? How rude of him!* A few more days pass, and then, just when you least expect it, you receive a phone call. It's your friend, apologizing for not calling back sooner, but reminding you that he had been out of town. You feel an arrow to your heart because you suddenly recall that he had asked you to water his plants. Your anger evaporates. You felt as though you had been abandoned, but your friend hadn't abandoned you. You just weren't paying attention.

As above, so below (see Matthew 6:10). From what we know about how things work here on earth, we have a good indication of God's ways. We have been given lots of clues and evidence about how God cares for us and is in it with us, no matter what.

HEALTH AND
THE ROSARY

Finding balance and maintaining overall health can seem daunting since managing stress, creating a calm environment, and maintaining good relationships require considerable effort and attention. By incorporating the Rosary into our daily routine, we draw closer to Jesus *and* foster peace and understanding, which reduces stress and enhances our physical, mental, and spiritual well-being.

Holistic health involves caring for the whole person—body, mind, and soul. This approach recognizes the physiological evidence that our physical health is interconnected with our mental and spiritual health. In praying the Rosary, we discover a unique way to bring spirit and body into alignment, thereby promoting overall health and harmony between physiological, psychological, and spiritual systems.

Before I go any further, I would like to say that praying the Rosary shouldn't be seen as a means to an end. It is first and foremost a way to spend time with God. It is also a meditative practice, and as such it is calming and centering. The repetitive nature of the prayers creates a rhythmically soothing experience, similar to deep breathing and other relaxation techniques prescribed by many physicians to combat obsessive worrying. The recitation of the Hail Marys, Our Fathers, and Glory Bes encourages us to enter a state of peaceful reflection, which helps to quiet the clamor. And at the end of the day, isn't that part of what religion offers? One of the blessings of religion is the gift of finding order and meaning in a world that often feels completely out of whack.

Unlike other prayers, through the act of holding the beads as markers of Christ's journey, the Rosary prayers provide a tactile connection to our faith. This tangible aspect of praying shifts our attention to the here and now and grounds us in the present moment. It's in the *combination of* the saying of the prayers and the holding of the beads that we open ourselves in a unique way to God's unconditional, empowering, redemptive love.

What exactly does all of that mean?

The Rosary is a unique spiritual experience because it intertwines prayer, meditation, and physical touch in a way that transcends ordinary religious practices. The tactile sensation of the beads, the repetitive articulation of the prayers, and the mental focus on the mysteries of Christ's life create a multisensory environment that encourages deep spiritual engagement. This unique blend helps bring to life a sacred space where we are able to experience a far-reaching connection with God, which in turn facilitates a sense of peace and spiritual rejuvenation.

Praying the Rosary also opens pathways to healing by emphasizing spiritual surrender. In this practice, we entrust our worries, fears, and burdens to God and allow faith to guide our lives. This act of surrender is mirrored in the teachings of the New Testament. As Paul writes in Philippians 4:6–7, "Do not worry about anything, but in everything by prayer and supplication with thanksgiving let your requests be made known to God. And the peace of God, which surpasses all understanding, will guard your hearts and your minds in Christ Jesus." By calling shotgun and putting God in the driver's seat, we acknowledge that we are not in control, which can be incredibly liberating and healing. Plus, we get to see all the scenery we miss because we're usually the one whose eyes are focused on the road ahead.

I love this quote attributed to Anselm of Canterbury: "I do not seek to understand in order that I may believe, but rather, I believe in order that I may understand." In other words, we need to let go and let our faith in Jesus guide us. When we do this, we enter into the process of spiritual healing, which leads to transformation. When we pray the Rosary, we engage in an act of faith that opens us to divine grace and fosters an inner healing that can bring comfort, clarity, and strength in times of trial and need.

PHYSICAL, MENTAL, AND SPIRITUAL WELL-BEING

The benefits of praying the Rosary extend beyond immediate stress relief. Regularly incorporating the Rosary into our daily routine can promote long-term physical, mental, and spiritual health. Not only can praying and meditating on the Rosary lower stress levels, they can also reduce the risk of stress-related health issues. And anyone who is suffering from high blood pressure, heart disease, or an anxiety disorder knows that the reduction of stress is key to improving one's health. Just as Jesus's embodiment of healing and wholeness attracts people to him, so, too, does the restorative potential of time spent in prayerful contemplation draw people to the Rosary.

The Rosary paves the way toward a more reflective, contemplative mindset, one capable of maintaining poise and equilibrium under even the most challenging of conditions. This mindset of detachment from the chaos that roils all around allows us to remain in the presence of God, a place where thoughts and emotions are processed in deeply personal ways. Clarity of mind inevitably leads to increased energy, improved decision-making, healthier interpersonal relationships, and a more Jesus-centric outlook on life.

Spiritually, the Rosary offers a way to deepen our relationship with God that is uniquely meaningful. When we spend time contemplating the essence of Jesus's life, we cannot help but internalize the core truths of our faith. The practice of praying the Rosary enlightens us about how we might emulate the virtues of both Jesus and Mary, as well as how to cultivate patience, compassion, and forgiveness in our lives. I'm reminded of the advice given by author and poet Rainer Maria Rilke: "Be patient toward all that is unsolved in your heart and try to love the *questions themselves*."[6] Our hearts are sometimes slow to reveal their woundedness. But with the

Rosary, we exemplify patience in in our prayer. Our actions prove our trust. Trust in the process. Trust that God is present even when we are feeling confusion, or the passage of time, or pain.

CONSCIOUSNESS AND SPIRITUAL AWARENESS

Understanding and deepening our spiritual awareness is a crucial aspect of living a fulfilled, meaningful, and impactful life. We strive to connect with God on a meaningful level, seeking always to understand God's will and presence as it manifests in our lives. We discover what it means to be a child of God when we deliberately and intentionally choose to expand our field of consciousness by embracing the sacred through Scripture, through prayer, through honoring our commitments, and through practicing what we preach.

But what do I mean by consciousness? Theorists propose different explanations for the awareness we call consciousness. For example, materialists will say that consciousness is a physical phenomenon of awareness caused by the brain's neurochemistry. Those who see the world as transcending strictly physical boundaries elect for a different understanding: consciousness (in other words, God), has always existed, and we are all creations of that consciousness. Said another way, you and I have been thought into existence through consciousness. We don't create it; we participate in it. As the writer of the Gospel of John states, "In the beginning was the

Word, and the Word was with God, and the Word was God" (John 1:1). Or, if the Word of God is the *Logos*, then we are the written characters of the Word of God.

The purpose of offering these theories is not to explore the nature of consciousness but to provide a basic definition that will shed a little light on the power of prayer. Let's say that consciousness is awareness (God) and the more we can grow in awareness (again, God), the more we can experience and the more we can participate in helping awareness (that is, God) create heaven on earth. In other words, consciousness (awareness) is universal and fundamental, and as such it involves recognizing a reality beyond our immediate physical existence; it involves connecting with a higher power, or truth, or fundamental essence. Some of us know this higher reality as God; for us, spiritual awareness tracks and reflects the ongoing process of opening our hearts and minds to the presence and guidance of God.

However, when we worry for extended periods, we cut ourselves off from God.

In the Sermon on the Mount, Jesus offers us healing advice when he says, "So do not worry about tomorrow, for tomorrow will bring worries of its own. Today's trouble is enough for today" (Matthew 6:34). Worry is a form of fear, which is a necessary part of life. It's programmed into our DNA as a survival mechanism. It's good to fear a hot stove or a busy intersection. Fear puts us on heightened alert and prevents us from getting hurt or killed. But fear can also manifest as anger, anxiety, or depression. Worry, which is nothing more than anxious anticipation of the future, is not necessarily in itself a bad thing. Worrying about a presentation at work, an upcoming doctor's appointment, or paying your bills on time may actually help you organize your thoughts so that you are prepared to handle these situations.

It's when worry leads to excessive stress that we have a problem. Then worry affects us mentally, spiritually, and biologically, since worry can lead to the creation of plaques in our blood and brain tissue, literally closing off the open pathways necessary for survival. Similarly, worry acts to clog the "arteries" of our spiritual connection to God. Jesus's advice, "Do not worry," is not to be taken as an easy platitude, a throwaway line, but as a critical clue to how we can facilitate the healing process of body, mind, and soul.

The Rosary, then, provides a unique pathway to consciousness by deepening our spiritual awareness, as well as a way of substituting faith for fear, because praying it requires a shift of focus away from what's vexing our minds to something sacred. Something special.

God calls us to heal the world, and we can do that by allowing ourselves to be healed. Healing begins within, through resting the body and the mind, and a healed person is a strong person, a focused person, a person who lives at a higher level of respect, insight, and love. We all have the potential to contribute to global healing. One of the ways we can do so is by resting and not contributing to the problems of the world though our worries or anxieties. Our interconnectedness means that each healed soul can positively influence countless others, creating a ripple effect of compassion and understanding. By addressing our own woundedness and seeking God's grace in dealing with it, we become instruments of his peace, capable of extending healing and hope to those around us. As St. Augustine writes, "Our hearts are restless until they rest in you." In rest, we find healing via unity with God.

Of course, resting can often be seen as laziness, especially when we look around and see that there is so much that seemingly needs to be done to bring healing to our earth. Living in a heavily populated world presents both challenges and opportunities. In 1900, there were nearly two billion people on this planet; today, we are a world of just over eight billion, which means that we have nearly four times as many opportunities for suffering as did our ancestors. The scale of problems may differ from those of the early twentieth century, but the magnitude of potential trauma certainly has increased. Yet, along with these challenges come eight billion chances to bring joy, comfort, and healing.

By getting ourselves in order spiritually, mentally, and physically, we reduce the collective burden of suffering by initiating a transformation that aligns us with God's purpose. In essence, healing ourselves is not just about personal wellbeing; it's about fulfilling our role in God's plan to heal the world, one person at a time.

MEDITATING ON THE MYSTERIES

As we meditate on the Joyful, Sorrowful, Glorious, and Luminous Mysteries, we enter into a contemplative state where we encounter God in a soul-opening way. This prayerful meditation involves more than simply the recitation of prayers; it demands that we fully engage our minds and hearts in the events we are contemplating, thus opening an entry point to a higher state of consciousness.

When reflecting on the Annunciation, we might ponder Mary's openness to God's will as an indication of her deep faith. This contemplation can inspire us to seek greater openness and trustfulness in our own lives. Similarly, meditating on the Passion of Christ might lead to a deeper understanding of Jesus's sacrifice and love, which in turn might inspire us to respond with gratitude and commitment. The practice of meditating on the Rosary's Mysteries enhances our spiritual awareness by focusing our attention on the divine narrative. We can see our own lives in the light of Christ's life, death, and resurrection. We cannot help but ask, *When have I experienced joy? Sorrow? Illumination? Glory or celebration?* When considering life through this spiritual perspective, we can appreciate God's immanent presence, influence, guidance, and action in our lives. The result is a vibrant relationship with God.

As we meditate on the Rosary, we are reminded of the humility, patience, compassion, and love exemplified by Jesus and Mary. When we realize how they were able to rise above the difficulties and downright ugliness in life, these virtues feel less like abstract ideals, more like tangible, attainable, practical strategies for living our lives. Through the transformative formula of contemplation plus prayer plus meditation, we fully appreciate the acts of healing and consolation that Mary and Jesus offer the world. With this awareness, we carry into our days an alertness for opportunities to do the same.

PRACTICAL STEPS TO ENHANCE SPIRITUAL AWARENESS

To fully benefit from the Rosary as a tool for deepening spiritual awareness, it is helpful to approach praying the Rosary with intentionality and reverence. Here are some practical steps.

1. **Dedicate Time.** Choose a specific time each day to pray the Rosary, creating a routine that allows for uninterrupted reflection and meditation.

2. **Create a Sacred Space.** Find a quiet place where you can focus on your prayers without distractions. You might consider setting up a small prayer corner with a crucifix, images of Jesus and Mary, or other devotional items.

3. **Engage with the Mysteries.** As you pray each decade, visualize the mystery, and place yourself in the scene. Then, consider the emotions and experiences of Jesus and Mary. Think about how they relate to your own life.

4. **Seek Spiritual Insights.** Reflect on what God might be revealing to you through each mystery. Ask the Holy Spirit to guide your thoughts and open your heart to deeper understanding.

5. **Journal Your Reflections.** After praying the Rosary, take a few minutes to write down insights or feelings that emerged during your meditation. This practice can help to solidify your spiritual growth and it will provide a record of your journey.

DAILY PRACTICES

In our quest for a balanced and fulfilling life, we cannot over-state the importance of daily practices. Daily practices are the foundation of a healthy lifestyle. They provide structure, promote consistency, and help us develop good habits such as gratitude. Just as physical health routines are essential for maintaining bodily wellness, spiritual disciplines are vital for nurturing our souls and strengthening our faith. These practices, including praying the Rosary, keep us grounded in our faith, promote healing, strengthen moments of reflection and prayer, and help us maintain our connection to God amid the busyness of daily life.

Setting aside specific times each day for prayer creates a rhythm that brings structure and balance to our lives. For example, praying the Rosary in the morning can set a tranquil tone for the day ahead, while praying in the evening allows time to reflect on the day's events and find restful ease in God's presence. Encouraging family members or friends to join you in praying the Rosary builds a supportive community of faith. Sharing this practice with others cements personal bonds at the same time that it creates a collective spiritual resilience.

The Rosary is traditionally prayed with specific mysteries assigned to different days of the week: the Joyful Mysteries on Mondays and Saturdays, the Sorrowful Mysteries on Tuesdays and Fridays, the Glorious Mysteries on Wednesdays and Sundays, and the Luminous Mysteries on Thursdays. However, your relationship with God through this devotional is deeply personal, and you should not feel strictly bound to this schedule. The Church believes that praying in this order helps deepen one's faith, but if you feel moved by the Spirit to focus on a particular set of mysteries, trust your discerning soul and the pressing realities of your life to guide you in your prayer journey.

To fully benefit from the daily practice of praying the Rosary, it is helpful to create a schedule that incorporates it into different parts of the day. Here are some suggestions for integrating the Rosary into day-to-day life.

MORNING PRAYER

Starting the day with the Rosary can set a positive tone and provide spiritual grounding. As we begin the day, morning prayer helps focus our minds and hearts on God's presence and also helps us to discern God's guidance. This is the perfect time to seek strength and grace for the challenges that lie ahead, and then offer up the day to God.

Suggested Practice
- Set aside ten to fifteen minutes each morning for the Rosary.

- Find a quiet place where you can pray without interruptions.
- Reflect on the Joyful Mysteries, contemplating the beginning of Jesus's life and the hope and promise it heralds.

MIDDAY PRAYER

Incorporating the Rosary into the middle of the day can serve as a spiritual refreshment that helps us pause, reflect, and reorient our focus. This is an opportunity to take a break from the busyness of work, daily chores, study, or service to others so that we can reconnect with God's peace.

Suggested Practice
- Take a short break during lunch or in the afternoon to pray a decade of the Rosary.
- Reflect on the Luminous Mysteries, which highlight key moments in Jesus's active ministry and timeless teachings.

EVENING PRAYER

Ending the day with the Rosary allows us to reflect on the events of the day, seek insight into and forgiveness for our shortcomings, and express gratitude for God's blessings. Evening prayer helps bring a sense of closure and it brings peace, both of which are essential in preparing us for restful sleep.

Suggested Practice

- Dedicate time before bedtime to pray the Rosary.
- Focus on the Glorious Mysteries, celebrating Jesus's Resurrection and the hope of eternal life.

Integrating the Rosary into our daily routine offers numerous spiritual benefits. It helps us develop a habit of regular prayer, which fosters a deeper relationship with God. Don't we grow closer to our beloved by spending time together? As mentioned earlier, the Rosary's meditative nature can also reduce stress, promote inner peace, and provide clarity and focus. By making the Rosary a part of our daily life, we create a rhythm of spiritual discipline that supports our faith journey and enhances our overall well-being.

PRACTICAL TIPS FOR MAINTAINING A ROSARY ROUTINE

Set Reminders. Use alarms or reminders on your phone to prompt you to pray the Rosary at designated times.

Create a Sacred Space. Designate a quiet area in your home for prayer, a place where you can keep your Rosary, Bible, a crucifix, and other devotional items.

Involve Family Members. Encourage your family to join you in praying the Rosary. Some families and community groups follow a call-and-answer practice.

Modeled on sessions where clergy lead by reciting aloud the first portion of each prayer and the other people in the group "answer" by reciting the concluding portions, this is a great way to pray the Rosary with your loved ones. Allowing everyone to have their turn as leader will keep even the youngest engaged and motivated. After all, who among us doesn't love having a chance to settle into a position of leadership when a sphere of safety has been created by the love and sincerity that surrounds?

Be Flexible. If your schedule is hectic, find creative ways to make the Rosary part of your day. You can pray during your commute, while receiving a medical treatment, preparing a meal, or walking your dog. You can combine your need to be in nature by praying the Rosary while sitting beneath a favorite tree or hiking a favorite trail. If you are a gardener, take your beads outside and meditate in the sacred realm of the small miracles you are cultivating.

While these are just some simple suggestions, I have found that all of these ideas have helped me elevate my prayer life, which in turn has had positive impacts on my day-to-day life. For more ideas to take with you on your spiritual journey, you might want to check out my book *MicroShifts: Transforming Your Life One Step at a Time.*[7]

UNDERSTANDING INFLAMMATION, BOTH PHYSICAL AND SPIRITUAL

Recently, researchers and medical professionals have increasingly focused their research efforts on better understanding inflammation, which is a complex biological response to the body's natural defense against pathogens such as bacteria and viruses. While often viewed negatively, inflammation plays a crucial role in healing. For instance, when you scratch your skin on something abrasive, healthy white blood cells release chemicals to prevent harmful substances from entering your bloodstream. Without inflammation, our bodies would be unable to fight off infections and heal wounds.

Severe complications arise when inflammation becomes chronic. Studies indicate that chronic inflammation can lead to cancer, debilitating arthritis, heart attacks, and autoimmune diseases, in which the body attacks its own tissue as if it was foreign. The reasons for this interplay are not fully understood, though genetics, stress response, diet, and lifestyle all play a role.

SPIRITUAL INFLAMMATION: THE RESPONSE OF THE MIND AND THE SOUL

What does this have to do with spirituality, with the Rosary? Good question.

Just as our bodies can react to injury with a protective process such as inflammation, our souls can react to stress and worry with patterned, habitual responses. We might have an argument with a friend and feel irritated. We may lose a loved one and feel immense sadness. We may suffer insomnia when we are worried about finances. In these ways, the feelings and the emotions that arise can be seen as natural responses to the spiritual threats, fissures, punctures, cuts, and bruises we experience as part of living our lives. These emotions perform the function of signals, alerting us that something is wrong and needs our attention.

Similar to the way a splinter lodged deep in a fingertip eventually works its way to the surface, pushed forward by forces inside, so, too, can a crying spell help release pressure around inflamed, hurtful emotions buried deep inside. Emotional responses are natural. Problems arise not when we *feel* sadness or disappointment or loneliness but when those emotional (and spiritual) reactions and feelings turn *chronic*. To stretch an analogy that concluded our discussion about Learning to Hear God's Voice, we cannot help but see that *as above, so below*. It's not quite so obvious that the same dynamic is true from the outside to the inside. When something going on in our little corner of the world festers inside, our mind (and heart) can turn inward against itself. Bessel van der Kolk, author of the compelling and thought-provoking bestseller *The Body Keeps the Score*, a book that explores the effects of trauma on physical and mental well-being, once stated, "As long as you keep secrets and suppress information, you are fundamentally at war with yourself."[8] Praying the Rosary provides a sacred space where we allow ourselves to confront hidden struggles and, with God's grace, begin the process of healing. When fear, anger, and anxiety shadow us everywhere we go, in everything we do, we absorb that negative influence into our physiology, our psychology, and our spirituality. This is when it seems as if worry and stress are running the show. Repressed emotions and unacknowledged disappointments can lead to a form of spiritual indigestion. *As on the outside, so on the inside.*

SPIRITUAL DIGESTION: PROCESSING LIFE'S EXPERIENCES

Our best spiritual health occurs when we properly digest our experiences. Just as proper digestion involves taking the best nutrients from our food and allowing the waste to pass through, we should process our experiences spiritually in a similar fashion. We experience something (e.g., someone cuts us off in traffic), take the nutrients from that experience (recognizing that someone misbehaved but choosing not to respond in kind), and let the rest pass away (feeling grateful that nothing serious happened, and looking forward to seeing your family at dinner).

However, sometimes an event gets firmly lodged in us, either because of pain, fear, hurt feelings, or trauma—something that challenges our survival or sense of who we are. This is especially true of events that happen during childhood. As author Antoine de Saint-Exupéry wisely observes in my all-time favorite book, *The Little Prince*, "Only the children know what they are looking for," said the little prince. "They devote their time to a rag doll and it becomes very important to them; and if anybody takes it away from them, they cry . . ."[9]

Early experience traumas show up in adult life in countless ways. Suddenly, the person who cut you off on the highway isn't just a stranger who made a bad decision but someone who reaffirms a defeatist attitude that you're always being taken advantage of. When we don't properly digest an event, either by putting it in its proper perspective or by not taking things personally, a spiritual version of IBS (irritable bowel syndrome) can take place. This leads to spiritual bloating that makes us feel uncomfortable, sluggish, unfocused, and ill-tempered.

God doesn't want us to be bloated in our faith. Often, we cling to outdated viewpoints simply because they're familiar. We fear the unknown. The future. And we recoil from situations that awaken negative memories.

But Jesus is reassuring. *Do not be afraid*, he says. *Don't worry*, he says. Over and over again he tells us, *I will care for you, I will feed you, I will clothe you*. By praying the Rosary and placing ourselves in the presence of Jesus and Mary, we grow to believe that these words are truths spoken to us from across millennia, across time and space. With promises like these as our support network, we have enough confidence to release the spiritual and emotional blockages that impede our connection with the divine.

Of course, this might sound as if it's easier said than done. And it is. Over the years, I've realized that there's not much I can do when it comes to growing closer to God except to show up, be honest, and express what's going on in my life. The rest is grace—grace for the moment and grace for the future. As much as I'd love to say that I feel transformed every time I pray the Rosary, I can't. Sometimes I feel nothing. Sometimes I feel annoyed. Sometimes I fall asleep.

But all is grace, or at least holds the potential for grace, and the more we show up, the more we grow in awareness that grace is here, now. We just need to be present to receive it. In many ways, grace is like one of those raffles at an Elk's lodge event. If you're not present, you miss out on the opportunity for big winnings if your number is called. So, sit still as much as you can, be as focused as is humanly possible, and do your best to be present. There's no secret formula for spiritual development other than to simply show up.

HEALING

In times of illness, distress, or hardship, it is natural that we seek sources of consolation, healing, and comfort. The Rosary is a uniquely potent tool perfectly designed to further spiritual and emotional healing. The Rosary is also a genuinely respectful way to seek heavenly intercession for health and well-being. The Rosary not only stimulates a deep connection with God but also serves as a channel through which we can seek divine intervention for ourselves and others. Integrating the focus on healing with the intercessory nature of the Rosary positions us to experience its transformative power in our lives.

Healing is a multifaceted process that encompasses physical, emotional, and spiritual dimensions. The Rosary, through its meditative prayers and reflections on the mysteries of Christ's life, offers a holistic approach to healing that addresses all three aspects. In the previous chapter, I referenced Bessel van der Kolk's important work on traumatic stress, which goes to the heart of my premise. Kolk puts his finger on an essential healing property of the Rosary when he explains that feeling safe with others is of vital significance to mental health: "Being able to feel safe with other people is probably the single most important aspect of mental health."[10] When we pray the Rosary, we connect to Jesus and Mary in a safe and sacred space where healing can occur.

SPIRITUAL HEALING

The Rosary provides spiritual healing by drawing us closer to God and helping us reflect on the fundamental truths of our faith. As we meditate on the mysteries, we are reminded of God's love, mercy, and redemptive power. This reflection can bring about an experience of spiritual renewal, helping us overcome feelings of despair, guilt, or spiritual dryness. Through regular prayer, the Rosary strengthens our faith and trust in God's providence, thereby fostering a deep sense of spiritual well-being.

For me, the Rosary has been a spiritual lifeline many times over the years. Growing up in a dysfunctional family, where alcoholism cast a long shadow over our home, I've carried some of that darkness into adulthood. One of the by-products of that upbringing is a persistent insecurity about the future. This is not uncommon. Many of us struggle with similar anxieties, especially in a world where the only certainty is uncertainty. For me, these worries have often led to intense bouts of insomnia, as I find it difficult to shut off my mind.

A few years ago, I began praying the Rosary before bed. At first, it wasn't helpful—my mind kept racing, mostly with thoughts about whether I was living up to my responsibilities as a father, husband, worker, and friend. But I persisted, and within a week, I found a rhythm. Being in the presence of Mary and Jesus during those prayers started to ease the fears that challenged my faith. Not only did my anxiety lessen, but I also began sleeping better. I woke up less frequently in the night, and sometimes I even woke up in the morning still quietly repeating the words of the Our Father or Hail Mary—a pretty wonderful way to start the day.

EMOTIONAL HEALING

The repetitious and rhythmic nature of praying the Rosary has a calming effect on the mind as anxiety and stress gradually lessen their grip on our thoughts, feelings, mood, and outlook. The act of praying the Rosary provides a structured time for introspection and emotional release, allowing us to process our feelings in the presence of God. Reflecting on the sorrows and joys of Jesus and Mary can also spark a sense of solidarity and comfort, as we are reminded that we are not alone in our struggles. The gift of emotional healing cultivates inner peace and resilience.

I'd like to tell you a story that captures how prayer has brought me a sense of calm during times of tragedy and loss.

On September 11, 2001, I stood in line at a Duane Reade pharmacy in Midtown Manhattan. In my hands were a couple of Snickers bars, a large bottle of water, a pair of children's safety scissors, and insoles for the dress shoes I wore that day. Fifteen minutes earlier, I had been standing in Times Square, watching as the South Tower of the World Trade

Center crumbled after the worst terrorist attack in United States history. Like everyone else, I was in a state of shock. One moment I was at work, and the next, I was part of a mass exodus of commuters fleeing from Manhattan, now a war zone, by crossing one of the many bridges leading to Long Island or New Jersey.

The memory is vivid: The store was buzzing with activity. Men and women in business attire hurried through the aisles, grabbing essentials from the shelves. Having been a Boy Scout for a few years—and perhaps just out of common sense—I stopped into the store to gather supplies for what could be a twenty-mile walk home.

At the checkout, a young woman, maybe twenty, stood behind the counter. A set of rosary beads hung around her neck. As she scanned my items with one hand, I noticed the other clutching a bead, her lips moving in silent prayer— Spanish, I think. When I reached for my receipt, I said, "God bless you." She met my gaze with eyes that were swimming in tears.

A few minutes later, I found myself at the intersection of 42nd Street and 5th Avenue, just outside the New York Public Library. Looking downtown, I could see the North Tower engulfed in fire and smoke. A crowd had gathered, all of us staring, transfixed by the destruction. Though nearly five miles away, the tower loomed large. I watched as it slowly descended, vanishing in silence, like snow falling on a hushed winter's night.

My body tensed. For a moment, I felt as if I had gone deaf. The world around me fell away. To my left, a woman screamed in what felt like a vacuum. To my right, I could see that a man was shouting, but I heard nothing. I stood there, frozen, as if under a spell. The spell broke only when F-15 warplanes roaring overhead restored my hearing with a sudden, jarring pop.

I reached inside the plastic bag of items I had just purchased, ripped open the package of insoles, and quickly cut them to the correct size with the safety scissors. As I slipped the padding into my dress shoes, I was aware of the surreal incongruity of standing on 5th Avenue in my socks. I looked down at the red handle of the scissors and then up at the billowing ash that had begun to mushroom against the blue sky. Quietly, to myself, I murmured the word *Safety*. I turned and began walking north toward the 59th Street Bridge. My thoughts drifted toward my wife and sons and what the future was going to hold, and then to all the people who may or may not have died as those building fell. And I thought back to the cashier and her rosary beads. As I walked, one confused and sorrowing human being surrounded by thousands of others, I began to pray the Rosary on my fingertips, one finger, one bead. In those moments, during that long journey from Manhattan to Long Island, I felt both connected to my fellow pilgrims whose lives were irrevocably changed and, curiously and inexplicably, I felt entirely alone—alone but for the quiet companionship brought to me by prayer.

PHYSICAL HEALING

While the primary focus of the Rosary is spiritual, many believe in its power to bring about physical healing as well. Through the intercession of Mary, we can seek God's help for physical ailments and conditions. The Rosary serves as a means of placing our trust in God's healing power as we ask for his intervention during times of illness and suffering. Many have found solace and hope in praying the Rosary for physical healing, experiencing improvements in their health and well-being.*

Years ago, a close friend of mine was diagnosed with a serious illness. Doctors were unsure of the outcome, and fear loomed large in her life. She turned to the Rosary, praying daily for strength and healing. Over time, not only did she find the courage to face her condition but she also experienced an improvement in her health. We have spoken about this numerous times over the years, and while we understand that medical science played a crucial role, we both believe that the peace and strength she received through the Rosary contributed significantly to her recovery.

And while this story might be anecdotal, here's a little science to back it up. According to studies conducted by researchers at the Mayo Clinic, meditation relaxes the body and can lower stress levels, reduce inflammation, regulate

---

* It is important to remember that spiritual practices should not replace medical treatment or professional healthcare advice. Always consult a doctor and follow prescribed medical treatments.

hormones, and strengthen the immune system.[11] Simply put, spending time meditating on the infinite gifts of God works wonders in every aspect of life.

As we reduce stress through prayer and meditation, our body repairs itself. Since stress has a major negative impact on our health, jobs, and relationships, by sincerely turning our concerns over to a power greater than ourselves, we can improve our physical health which—neatly but unsurprisingly, given what we know about God's foresight—also helps us psychologically.

Thus, while it's not for me to say that the Rosary will lead to miraculous healings, praying this beautiful prayer contains within it the marvelously powerful potential to upgrade our well-being simply by alleviating our bodies from the deleterious effects of stress.

BREATHING THE ROSARY

O ne aspect of our physiological processes directly linked to meditations like the Rosary relates to the vagus nerve. The vagus nerve is the longest cranial nerve in the body. It plays a crucial role in the regulation of the parasympathetic nervous system. The parasympathetic nervous system promotes the "rest and digest" state that counteracts the "fight or flight" response, which is governed by the sympathetic nervous system. Think of the parasympathetic nervous system as a parachute that safely guides you to earth after the sympathetic nervous system tosses you from an airplane.

Originating in the brain stem, the vagus nerve extends through the neck and thorax down to the abdomen and connects to various organs, including the heart, lungs, and digestive tract. Understanding the physiological role of this nerve sheds light on how spiritual practices like praying the Rosary can impact our well-being.

FUNCTIONS OF THE VAGUS NERVE

Regulation of Heart Rate. The vagus nerve helps to lower the heart rate by transmitting signals that counteract the stimulating effects of the sympathetic nervous system.

Digestive Processes. The vagus nerve aids in stimulating digestion and regulating the function of the digestive tract.

Respiratory Rate. The vagus nerve helps control the rate of involuntary bodily functions like breathing. We can help the vagus nerve do its job more efficiently by intentionally focusing on our breathing.

Inflammatory Response. The vagus nerve assists in modulating the immune response to inflammation.

Stimulation of the vagus nerve can enhance parasympathetic activity, leading to a state of relaxation and improved physical health, including reduction of stress hormones, lowering of blood pressure, and enhancement of digestive and immune functions. And these life-changing effects are simply a breath away.

WHAT IS VAGAL BREATHING?

Vagal breathing refers to specific breathing techniques designed to stimulate the vagus nerve and enhance parasympathetic nervous system activity. These breathing techniques involve slow, deep breathing patterns that promote relaxation and reduce stress.

KEY TECHNIQUES IN VAGAL BREATHING

Diaphragmatic Breathing. Deep breathing that engages the diaphragm, which allows the lower lungs to fill with air. This technique both enhances oxygen exchange and stimulates the vagus nerve.

Slow Breathing. Reducing the number of breath cycles per minute (typically to five or six) can help the vagus nerve do its job and also promote a state of calm and balance.

Breath Counting. Counting breaths during inhalation and exhalation can help lower heart rate and blood pressure.

Throughout the years, I've used structured breathing patterns for all kinds of situations. When I am going to give a speech or presentation, when I am being interviewed on the radio or on a television show, when I am about to teach a class, and when I am facing any potentially upsetting situation, I rely on structured breathing to calm my nerves and center my thoughts. I also use breathing techniques to prepare for spiritual practice.

What I find so intriguing is the paradox of control. If we really think about it, we don't have a lot of direct control over our bodies. Yes, we can outwardly move our arms and legs, blink our eyes, and express ourselves through speech, writing, or sign language. But we can't directly create bile in our liver, or force our digestive system to break down our food, or command our lungs to stop breathing. And yet, when we focus on our breath, we do gain a not-insignificant amount of control. Through focused breathing, we can influence the internal workings of our bodies. One way of looking at this intentional proactive breathing practice is that it allows us to drive the bus of our lives rather than getting on a bus that's being driven by someone else.

Since I have found certain techniques to be so very helpful in preparing for spiritual practice, I am going to share with you my suggestions for using these techniques as you cultivate your own regular routine and relationship with the Rosary. I hope that my strategies help you as much as they help me.

DEEP BREATHING WITH EACH BEAD

- In between each prayer, and as you move through each bead of the Rosary, take a deep breath in through your nose for a count of four. Hold for a count of four. Exhale through your mouth for a count of six.
- On each bead, synchronize your breathing with a short prayer prayed between each Hail Mary and Our Father. For example, as you inhale, think or say, "Lord Jesus Christ," and as you exhale, think or say, "have mercy on me." Then, enter into your regular prayer cycle.

- Before starting each decade, practice box breathing. Inhale for a count of four, hold for four, exhale for four, and pause for another four. Repeat this cycle three times.
- While praying each Hail Mary, focus on diaphragmatic breathing. Practice now by placing one hand on your chest and the other on your abdomen. Breathe deeply so that your abdomen rises more than your chest. This is the breathing technique taught to young singers by choir directors all over the world. With practice, diaphragmatic breathing will become second nature to you.

Reducing breath cycles through deep, slow breathing ushers the body into a more relaxed state. Fewer, deeper breaths allow for better oxygen exchange in the lungs, enhancing blood oxygen levels and promoting overall health. This technique lets the body shift from a sympathetic state to a parasympathetic state, thereby improving heart rate variability (HRV), which is the steadiness of your heartbeats, and also reducing stress-related symptoms.

Remember earlier when we talked about holistic medicine? Well, combining vagal breathing with praying the Rosary is a holistic approach to prayer that just makes sense. This integrative approach leverages the physiological benefits of deep, controlled breathing with the spiritual and mental benefits of meditative prayer.

Regular practice of deep diaphragmatic breathing improves HRV, which is a key marker of cardiovascular health and resilience. Improved HRV is associated with better stress management and overall heart health.[12] Obviously, then, praying the Rosary in a calm, repetitive manner complements the effects of vagal breathing and vice versa. The effects are the enhancement of HRV—and better cardiovascular health.

Vagal breathing strengthens the gut-brain axis (the network of communication between those two parts of the body), improving digestion and mental clarity. This connection is crucial for maintaining overall health and well-being.[13]

THE ROSARY
OF NATURE

We get so caught up in our daily lives that we often overlook the beauty and wonder of God's creation. But by contemplating the mysteries of the Rosary while experiencing the natural world, we can ground ourselves in our faith and, in the process, gain renewed appreciation for all the good people and the remarkable world we call home.

In the book of Genesis, we read that God created the heavens and the earth, bringing forth life in all its diversity and splendor. This creation reflects his glory, wisdom, artistry, and love. As we observe the elements of nature—the air we breathe, the warmth of the sun, the trees growing from the earth—we are reminded of God's continuous presence in the world he entrusted to our care.

The elements of water, air, fire, and earth, which are fundamental to life, can also serve as symbols of spiritual truths. Water has a strong spiritual connection to the rites of purification and renewal. Air represents the breath of life and the ongoing work of the Spirit. Fire signifies God's love, passion, the light of Christ, and the flame of the Sacred Heart of Jesus.

Earth symbolizes stability, nourishment, and the foundation of our faith. It is as children of the Garden—children of the earth—that we experience this life that God has bestowed upon us.

Let us turn now to how reflecting on these elements will enhance our understanding of the mysteries of the Rosary. When we immerse ourselves in the mysteries, we cannot help but emerge with a greater awareness of the immensity of God's plan, as well as new resolve to accept God's request that we lovingly care for and bring healing to his creation.

REFLECTING ON THE MYSTERIES OF THE ROSARY

Each of the mysteries we contemplate as we pray the Rosary provides a focal point that is genuinely relevant. It is relevant to each one of us, to the lives we are privileged to live, and to the world all around us. By integrating these reflections with our experience of one another and of nature, we inevitably draw closer to God, if for no other reasons than out of sheer admiration of, and gratitude and appreciation for, his creation.

JOYFUL MYSTERIES AND CREATION

While meditating on the Joyful Mysteries, we reflect on the new life and hope that God's creation brings. This happens through announcements, the birthing of new creation, and discovery, what writer Maura Poston calls "the hopefulness of regeneration," an allusion to the new life we can experience through our faith journey. Tradition holds that the Annunciation takes place in a home, the Visitation at the end of a journey on the road, the Nativity beneath the stars in a stable of animals, the Presentation in an architectural construct surrounded by a community of people, and the Finding in the Temple in a house of God, otherwise known as a place of people and tradition, words and promises, hopes and dreams. Each of these settings reveals aspects of God's plan as well as his devotion to and involvement in the world. As we walk through a garden or park, gather together as a family, celebrate a birth, bury our loved ones, educate and nurture our children, mentor young people finding their purpose in life, perform our duties and daily rituals, and pray together as a congregation, we cannot help but contemplate the beauty of new life, the interconnectedness of all living things, and the joy that comes from recognizing that we, too, are one of God's treasured creations. God put something brilliant in us that is unique in all the world, and he is counting on us to make him proud. We are one small but irreplaceable part of God's handiwork in all creation.

SORROWFUL MYSTERIES AND REDEMPTION

The Sorrowful Mysteries take us to the scene of Christ's Passion. And let us just pause for a moment to take this in. Let your mind imagine the human experience behind the sacrifices made on behalf of all of us, the suffering Jesus endured for the sake of our redemption. As we reflect on his suffering and death, we draw parallels with the struggles and challenges present in nature, such as the harshness of winter storms, the devastation wreaked by natural disasters, the mortal pain of illness and disease, or the inconsolable grief of losing a loved one. Heartfelt reflections like these deepen our awareness of Christ's suffering and sacrifice. What we take from a compassionate, empathetic meditation on Jesus's sacrifice is hopeful resilience in the face of our own personal trials.

GLORIOUS MYSTERIES AND NEW LIFE

The Glorious Mysteries celebrate the triumph of Jesus over death with nothing less than the promise of eternal life. As we meditate on the Resurrection, the Ascension, the Descent of the Holy Spirit, the Assumption of Mary, and the Coronation of Mary, we draw inspiration from the renewal and rebirth seen in nature mirrored in the cyclical recalibration of our perpetually fluctuating emotions, which can careen from wild happiness to crushing despondency—in every aspect of life, really. Knowing for sure that night ushers in a new dawn, and the storm always ends, and the tracks of tears always give way to smiles, strengthens our faith whether we are filled with joy and optimism or are struggling to see our way out of very hard times.

LUMINOUS MYSTERIES AND DIVINE LIGHT

The Luminous Mysteries highlight key moments in Jesus's ministry that reveal his divine nature. Reflecting on these mysteries while listening to the sounds of gurgling river water flowing downstream, or basking in the beauty of sunlight, or turning our gaze upward in wonder toward the starry night sky, can serve to remind us of the light of Christ that guides and illuminates our every step. There are blessings in everything we do, everything we are, every dream we dream. Praying the Rosary keeps us in touch with these truths.

ORGANIZING A NATURE WALK WITH THE ROSARY

To fully appreciate the connection between the elements of nature and the mysteries of the Rosary, consider organizing a nature walk during which you and your family and friends pray the Rosary while actively opening yourselves to experience and reflect on the limitless beauty of creation. Time spent in this way with people you love cannot help but be an experience that fosters a deeper connection with God and with the natural world.

STEPS FOR ORGANIZING A NATURE WALK

Choose a Scenic Location. Select a park, garden, or nature trail that offers a variety of natural sights and sounds. If you live in an urban area, you can pray the

Rosary while walking around your neighborhood. The point is that wonder and beauty are embedded in all of God's creation.

Set a Schedule. Plan the walk for a time of day when you are free from work or other duties, or when you know you are most in need of grace, or when the natural surroundings are particularly beautiful, such as in the early hours of morning or evening.

Begin with a Prayer. Begin the walk with a group prayer in which everyone asks God to bless their time together and open their hearts to his presence.

Reflect on the Mysteries. Pause at different points throughout the walk to pray a decade of the Rosary and reflect on the corresponding mystery. Use these interludes to allow everyone time to observe and contemplate the natural elements around them.

Share Reflections. Invite participants to share their thoughts and reflections at the end of the walk. Discuss how the experience of nature enhances our understanding of the mysteries and adds an extra-special dimension to our faith.

INTERCESSORY HEALING AND THE ROSARY

One of the significant aspects of the Rosary is the role it plays as a tool for intercession. When we pray the Rosary, we ask Mary, the mother of God, to intercede for us and present our petitions to her Son. This intercessory nature of the Rosary in effect allows us to bring our needs and the needs of others before God in our quest to seek his grace and mercy. By dedicating our prayers to specific intentions, we can ask for God's healing touch in our lives as well as in the lives of those we care about. Whether we are praying for ourselves, our family, our friends, or someone we have never even met, the Rosary provides a way to entrust our concerns to God's loving care.

SUGGESTED PRACTICES

- **Praying for Personal Healing.** Dedicate each decade of the Rosary to a specific aspect of healing (physical, emotional, or spiritual). Reflect on the mysteries. Ask for Mary's intercession in your healing process.

- **Praying for Others.** Offer the Rosary for the intentions of others who are in need of healing. Mention their names and their specific needs before you begin praying each decade. Ask that God's grace and mercy be upon them.
- **Healing Novena.** Consider praying a Rosary novena. A novena focuses on a particular intention for nine consecutive prayer days. Committing to and engaging in a sustained prayer such as a novena provides spiritual benefits akin to the physical benefits—more energy, sharpened mental faculties, and greater vitality—we experience from a specialized workout program adhered to with dedication.

IGNATIAN CONTEMPLATION AND THE POWER OF IMAGINATION IN PRAYER

For more than a decade, I have been fascinated with Ignatian spirituality, which is to say the teachings of St. Ignatius. It will take another book to describe the effect St. Ignatius's teachings have had on my life. Ignatian spirituality emphasizes the importance of using the imagination in prayer. Right away, just stating this one aspect of Ignatian spirituality, you know one significant effect it has had on me: it showed me the secret to praying a "better" Rosary!

St. Ignatius believed that we could experience the Gospel more personally by engaging our imagination as we read Scripture. This method of using one's imagination to connect with God is known as "Ignatian contemplation" or, alternatively, "composition of place," because it invites us to "place" ourselves in the scenes of the Gospel stories. As we shall see in the pages to come, each set of Rosary mysteries has a corresponding Bible passage.

By actively imagining ourselves side by side with Jesus, we experience the events in vivid, almost tangible ways. This imaginative engagement helps us internalize the truths of the Gospel. As we imagine Christ's smile, his touch, his emotions, or his voice as he speaks, we deepen our relationship with him and open our hearts to his transformative presence.

This practice moves us beyond mere intellectual understanding to a heartfelt encounter with the divine. The mysteries of faith come alive.

Ignatian contemplation involves several key elements:

- preparation: find a quiet place in which we can calm our minds;
- Scripture: read a chosen passage attentively;
- imagination: explore the physical setting employing all our senses to make it vivid and realistic;
- immersion: enter the scene as either a participant or an observer; and
- dialogue: dare to engage in dialogue with Jesus and other biblical characters.

After having immersed yourself in the scene, reflecting on the experience and its uniquely personal significance is essential. Closing the contemplation with a prayer of thanksgiving enables us to integrate the insights gained into our daily lives.

The rewards of Ignatian contemplation are rich in three overarching ways. First, it deepens our relationship with Jesus by enabling a more personal and intimate engagement with the Gospel stories. Ignatian contemplation also enhances our understanding of Scripture by bringing the biblical passages to life in a vivid and sensory way. Finally, Ignatian contemplation provides emotional and spiritual healing through experiencing Jesus's presence in our hearts.

When we reflect on how the Gospel stories relate to our own lives, Ignatian contemplation fosters the integration of faith into hearts and minds, which then moves into everyday experiences. We cannot help but encounter God in a deeply personal and transformative way.

USING YOUR IMAGINATION WITH THE ROSARY

One effective way to enrich your Rosary prayer is to use your imagination the way Ignatius taught us to do. After you begin meditating on a mystery, start imagining yourself in the scene. For instance, if you are contemplating the Annunciation, try to envision the moment Gabriel appeared to Mary. Is it morning or evening? Is the air cool or stagnant? Is the room sparsely furnished or homey and decorated? What is Mary wearing? Imagine what the angel may have looked like to her: was Gabriel a ray of light, or did he assume the figure of a man? What is Mary's physiological reaction when she receives the news? Is her heart beating wildly, or is she calm? What happens after the angel leaves? Continue the story, not necessarily with words but with images. Become fully present in the mystery. In essence, the challenge is to become *part of* the story. Then reflect on how the scene relates to your own life. In this case, it would be appropriate to consider what can be learned from Mary's unquestioning acceptance of the will of God.

Place yourself at the wedding at Cana. Maybe you are an invited guest turned curious observer as you overhear the brief exchange between Jesus and his mother. Look around at the people enjoying the celebration. Observe the servants: are they worried? After all, they know the drama that's going on behind the scenes, and this doesn't reflect well on their master, the host. Think of the excitement. Is there music? Are people laughing? Are people dancing? Knowing that wine is such an integral part of the celebration, think about what would happen if the wine ran out. How would the atmosphere change? Switching your focus to Christ, what is the expression on Jesus's face when he performs his first public miracle? On Mary's face? Then, imagine yourself holding a glass of the just-poured wine. What does it taste like? Allow your mind to contemplate the many miracles in your own life. Are there times when you can metaphorically change water into wine, flipping the perspective from hopeless to hopeful?

Imagine that you are a member of the cast at the Passion. Picture the brutality of the beatings. (If you're squeamish, maybe focus instead on scenes at the Garden of Gethsemane.) Imagine what Jesus might have looked like as the whips tear at his flesh. Feel his pain as he struggles to his feet after having been beaten. Ponder whether you would be able to endure this torture for God. Imagine what must have been going on in Christ's mind as he stands before the Romans. What is he feeling? What are the reactions of the Romans or the common people witnessing these events? How do you feel witnessing someone being treated like this? How would you feel if it was a friend of yours? How would you feel if it was an enemy? Then contemplate the meaning of suffering in your life.

Imagine being a gardener who is tending the area near Christ's tomb when the women come by early Sunday morning to anoint the body. You watch as the angel rolls away the stone. Then you hear the astonished, indescribably joyous shouts of the women as they marvel and celebrate. *He is risen!* What is your reaction? What is going on inside you? Do you join them in a noisy outburst, or is your joy a quiet surge that makes you understand the meaning of the phrase "my heart is full?" What is the reaction of the guards? Do you lean in to get a peek inside the tomb? What do you see? What do you feel—the coolness of a cave, or the stuffiness of an enclosed space? What is the morning like? Are there clouds in the sky? Are there birds in the trees? Do you hear birdsong, or are they so fascinated with the goings-on, all they can do is watch from above? Then bring your meditation back to Christ. Focus on his journey. His message. His example. His faith in the Father. Pray for a deeply felt understanding of the glory of the Resurrection. Consider: what does Christ's rising mean in your life?

See how easy it is? And how fascinating? Simply by using your imagination, you can make each of the mysteries meaningfully personal.

On a physical level, the more you can experience something, the more you feel moved by it. Christ, even in all his divinity, experienced the world in human ways. Like us, Jesus felt pain and hope and disappointment and betrayal and love and friendship. While keeping our eyes focused on the Good News of Christ, we can expand the stories personally through the realm of our imagination. The way I imagine Christ's smile is no doubt different from the way you imagine his smile, but that doesn't matter. What matters is that we enter into the scene, become part of God's Word, and attempt in our own human way to experience something of what he experienced.

HOW TO PRAY
THE ROSARY

This chapter provides a step-by-step guide to praying the Rosary, whether you are using traditional Rosary beads or your fingers.

1. Choose a set of mysteries that will be the focus of your prayers. Make the Sign of the Cross. Recite the Apostles' Creed while holding the crucifix in your fingers.

2. Move to the first bead. Pray the Our Father, also known as the Lord's Prayer.

3. On the next three beads, recite one Hail Mary for each bead while you meditate first on the virtue of faith, then hope, and finally charity.

4. Recite the Glory Be between the last of the three Hail Mary beads and the next bead.

5. On the following bead, say the Our Father and begin meditating on the first mystery.

6. Moving to your right (counterclockwise), begin praying the Hail Mary. Repeat this prayer for each bead.

7. After reciting a Hail Mary on each of the ten beads, recite the Glory Be. This completes the first decade.
8. Repeat steps 5 through 7 for each mystery.
    Conclude your Rosary with a Hail, Holy Queen.
9. Finish with the Sign of the Cross.

Let's return to the topic of worry for a moment. Worry is a silent killjoy, a blackout curtain that prevents the light from shining through to us. You may already know this in your heart, but just in case you don't, I offer the following as a gentle reminder: God is all around us, yet we often let worry and fear block our awareness of God. I want to leave you with these words from Christ's Sermon on the Mount. Keep these words in mind every minute of every day, whether you are praying the Rosary or simply living your life.

Therefore I tell you, do not worry about your life, what you will eat or what you will drink, or about your body, what you will wear. Is not life more than food, and the body more than clothing? Look at the birds of the air; they neither sow nor reap nor gather into barns, and yet your heavenly Father feeds them. Are you not of more value than they? And can any of you by worrying add a single hour to your span of life? And why do you worry about clothing? Consider the lilies of the field, how they grow; they neither toil nor spin, yet I tell you, even Solomon in all his glory was not clothed like one of these. But if God so clothes the grass of the field, which is alive today and tomorrow is thrown into the oven, will he not much more clothe you—you of little faith? Therefore, do not worry, saying, "What will we eat?" or "What will we drink?" or "What will we wear?" For it is the Gentiles who strive for all these things; and indeed your heavenly Father knows that you need all these things. But strive first for the kingdom of God and his righteousness, and all these things will be given to you as well.

So do not worry about tomorrow, for tomorrow will bring worries of its own. Today's trouble is enough for today.

—Matthew 6:25–34

THE CYCLE OF THE ROSARY

The Sign of the Cross
In the name of the Father, and of the Son, and of the Holy Spirit. Amen.

The Apostles' Creed
I believe in God, the Father almighty, Creator of heaven and earth, and in Jesus Christ, his only Son, our Lord, who was conceived by the Holy Spirit, born of the Virgin Mary, suffered under Pontius Pilate, was crucified, died and was buried; he descended into hell; on the third day he rose again from the dead; he ascended into heaven, and is seated at the right hand of God the Father almighty; from there he will come to judge the living and the dead. I believe in the Holy Spirit, the holy catholic Church, the communion of saints, the forgiveness of sins, the resurrection of the body, and life everlasting. Amen.

The Lord's Prayer
Our Father, who art in heaven, hallowed be thy name; thy kingdom come; thy will be done on earth as it is in heaven. Give us this day our daily bread, and forgive us our trespasses as we forgive those who trespass against us; and lead us not into temptation, but deliver us from evil. Amen.

Hail Mary

Hail Mary, full of grace, the Lord is with thee. Blessed are thou among women and blessed is the fruit of thy womb, Jesus. Holy Mary, Mother of God, pray for us sinners, now and at the hour of our death. Amen.

Glory Be to the Father

Glory Be to the Father and to the Son and to the Holy Spirit, as it was in the beginning, is now and ever shall be, world without end. Amen.

Hail, Holy Queen

Hail, Holy Queen, Mother of Mercy, our life, our sweetness and our hope. To thee do we cry, poor banished children of Eve. To thee do we send up our sighs, mourning and weeping in this valley of tears. Turn, then, most gracious advocate, thine eyes of mercy toward us, and after this exile show unto us the blessed fruit of thy womb, Jesus; O clement, O loving, O sweet Virgin Mary.

Jesus Prayer

Lord Jesus Christ, Son of the living God, have mercy on me, a sinner.

Sign of the Cross

In the name of the Father, and of the Son, and of the Holy Spirit. Amen.

THE
JOYFUL MYSTERIES

THE FIRST JOYFUL MYSTERY
The Annunciation

In the sixth month the angel Gabriel was sent by God to a town in Galilee called Nazareth, to a virgin engaged to a man whose name was Joseph, of the house of David. The virgin's name was Mary. And he came to her and said, 'Greetings favored one, The Lord is with you! . . .' The angel said to her, 'Do not be afraid, Mary, for you have found favor with God. And now, you will conceive in your womb and bear a son, and you will name him Jesus. . . .' The angel said to her, 'The Holy Spirit will come upon you, and the power of the Most High will overshadow you; therefore the child to be born will be holy; Son of God. . . .' Then Mary said, 'Here I am, the servant of the Lord; let it be with me according to your word.' Luke 1:26–28, 30–31, 35, 38

Reflection Questions

1. Imagine yourself in Mary's place, hearing the angel's message. What do you see around you? What sounds do you hear? What does this experience with an angel look like? Do you hear a rush of wind, or feel a change in the air all around you? How would you feel about being chosen for such a significant role in God's plan?

2. Reflect on Mary's response to the angel, "Here am I, the servant of the Lord." How might you adopt a similar attitude of trust and obedience in your own life?

THE SECOND JOYFUL MYSTERY
The Visitation

In those days Mary set out and went with haste to a Judean town in the hill country, where she entered the house of Zechariah and greeted Elizabeth. When Elizabeth heard Mary's greeting the child leaped in her womb. And Elizabeth was filled with the Holy Spirit and exclaimed with a loud cry, 'Blessed are you among women, and blessed is the fruit of your womb. . . . And blessed is she who believed that there would be a fulfillment of what was spoken to her by the Lord.' Luke 1:39–42, 45

Reflection Questions

1. Consider the journey Mary undertook to visit Elizabeth. How do you imagine the journey? What could have been some of the difficulties she experienced? What could have been some of the joys she felt as she went excitedly to see her cousin? How does the act of reaching out to others in their time of need reflect Christ's message that love is a verb?

2. Reflect on Elizabeth's recognition of Mary's faith. How does your faith help you to recognize and affirm the presence of Christ in others?

THE THIRD JOYFUL MYSTERY
The Nativity of Jesus

In those days a decree went out from Emperor Augustus that all the world should be registered. . . . All went to their own towns to be registered. Joseph also went from the town of Nazareth in Galilee to Judea, to the city of David called Bethlehem, because he was descended from the house and family of David. He went to be registered with Mary, to whom he was engaged and who was expecting a child. While they were there, the time came for her to deliver her child. And she gave birth to her firstborn son and wrapped him in bands of cloth, and laid him in a manger, because there was no place for them in the inn. Luke 2:1, 3–7

Reflection Questions

1. Imagine being present at the birth of Jesus in the humble surroundings of a stable. What thoughts and feelings arise as you witness this moment? Call to mind the overwhelming surge of emotions we experience at the birth of any child. Then try to put yourself in the humblest of surroundings, and a first-time mother has just given birth to a healthy baby boy. The scene is dreamlike, and you are deeply moved. Now imagine what it would be like to join Mary as she welcomes the child who would

change everything for everyone. Or imagine you are
Joseph. What does he experience as he looks upon
his son for the first time?

2. Reflect on the significance of God choosing to
enter the world in such a humble setting. How does
this influence your understanding of humility and
service?

THE FOURTH JOYFUL MYSTERY
The Presentation of the Infant Jesus in the Temple

After eight days had passed, it was time to circumcise the child; and he was called Jesus, the name given by the angel before he was conceived in the womb. . . . Now there was a man in Jerusalem whose name was Simeon; this man was righteous and devout, looking forward to the consolation of Israel, and the Holy Spirit rested on him. It had been revealed to him by the Holy Spirit that he would not see death before he had seen the Lord's Messiah. Guided by the Spirit, Simeon came into the temple; and when the parents brought in the child Jesus, to do for him what was customary under the law, he took him in his arms and praised God, saying, 'Master, now you are dismissing your servant in peace, according to your word; for my eyes have seen your salvation.' Luke 2:21, 25–30

Reflection Questions

1. Picture yourself in the temple with Simeon as he is holding the infant Jesus. Is he tender and in his own world, or is he excited and celebratory? What emotions and thoughts come to mind as you join Simeon in recognizing this baby as the Messiah? Who else looks on during this exchange? Consider

whether it matters at all what is going on in the temple when such a rare scene is happening right before your eyes.

2. Reflect on Simeon's words about seeing God's salvation. How do you see God's work and salvation in action in your own life today?

THE FIFTH JOYFUL MYSTERY
The Finding of Jesus in the Temple

Now every year his parents went to Jerusalem for the festival of the Passover. And when he was twelve years old, they went up as usual for the festival. When the festival was ended and they started to return, the boy Jesus stayed behind in Jerusalem, but his parents did not know it. Assuming that he was in the group of travelers, they went a day's journey. Then they started to look for him among their relatives and friends. When they did not find him, they returned to Jerusalem to search for him. After three days they found him in the temple, sitting among the teachers, listening to them and asking them questions. And all who heard him were amazed at his understanding and his answers. When his parents saw him they were astonished; and his mother said to him, 'Child, why have you treated us like this? Look, your father and I have been searching for you in great anxiety.' He said to them, 'Why were you searching for me? Did you not know that I must be in my Father's house?' Luke 2:41–49

Reflection Questions

1. Imagine the anxiety of Mary and Joseph as they searched for Jesus, and their relief when they found him in the temple. Can you relate their experience

to times of panic, fear, or feeling lost? Do you know what it feels like to be searching for some elusive thing, discovery, and reconnection in your own life?

2. Reflect on Jesus's words, "Did you not know that I must be in my Father's house?" Were these words of admonishment, or was he trying to be reassuring? How do these words inspire you to prioritize your relationship with God and seek his presence?

THE
LUMINOUS MYSTERIES

THE FIRST LUMINOUS MYSTERY
The Baptism of Jesus in the River Jordan

Then Jesus came from Galilee to John at the Jordan, to be baptized by him. . . . And when Jesus had been baptized, just as he came up from the water, suddenly the heavens were opened to him and he saw the Spirit of God descending like a dove and alighting on him. And a voice from heaven said, 'This is my Son, the Beloved, with whom I am well pleased.' Matthew 3:13, 16–17

Reflection Questions

1. Envision the scene at the Jordan River as Jesus is baptized. You are a witness as the Spirit of God descends upon Jesus. What does this look like? You hear the voice of God the Father rumbling from heaven. How do you feel? What are your thoughts? What do you do?

2. Reflect on the significance of God proclaiming Jesus as his beloved Son. How does this declaration shape your understanding of your own identity as a beloved child of God?

THE SECOND LUMINOUS MYSTERY
The Manifestation at Cana

On the third day there was a wedding in Cana of Galilee, and the mother of Jesus was there. Jesus and his disciples had also been invited to the wedding. When the wine gave out, the mother of Jesus said to him, 'They have no wine.' And Jesus said to her, 'Woman, what concern is that to you and to me? My hour has not yet come.' His mother said to the servants, 'Do whatever he tells you.' Now standing there were six stone water jars for the Jewish rites of purification, each holding twenty or thirty gallons. Jesus said to them, 'Fill the jars with water.' And they filled them up to the brim. He said to them, 'Now draw some out, and take it to the chief steward.' So they took it. When the steward tasted the water that had become wine, and did not know where it came from (though the servants who had drawn the water knew), the steward of the feast called the bridegroom and said to him, 'Everyone serves the good wine first, and then the inferior wine after the guests have become drunk. But you have kept the good wine until now.' Jesus did this, the first of his signs, in Cana of Galilee, and revealed his glory; and his disciples believed in him. John 2:1–11

Reflection Questions
1. Imagine being a guest at the wedding in Cana and witnessing Jesus perform his first miracle. Picture the hustle and bustle of the event. What do the

attendees look like? Is there music? Are the bride and groom aware of the crisis, or have they been shielded from knowing about it? Is the host calm and in control or is he panicky? What does the water taste like, what does the new wine taste like? How does this miracle deepen your understanding of Jesus's power and compassion?

2. Reflect on Mary's instruction to the servants, "Do whatever he tells you." How can her advice be applied in your own life, especially during times of uncertainty, peril, or need?

THE THIRD LUMINOUS MYSTERY
The Proclamation of the Kingdom of God

Now when Jesus heard that John had been arrested, he withdrew to Galilee. He left Nazareth and made his home in Caperum by the sea, in the territory of Zebulun and Naphtali, so that what had been spoken through the prophet Isaiah might be fulfilled: 'Land of Zebulun, land of Naphtali, on the road by the sea, across the Jordan, Galilee of the Gentiles—the people who sat in darkness have seen a great light, and for those who sat in the region and shadow of death light has dawned.' From that time Jesus began to proclaim, 'Repent, for the kingdom of heaven has come near.' Matthew 4:12–17

Reflection Questions

1. Imagine hearing Jesus proclaim, "Repent, for the kingdom of heaven has come near." What does Jesus's voice sound like? What do you experience when you hear these words? Does this clarion call to repentance inspire you to make changes in your life? What comes to mind as a good first step?

2. Reflect on the fulfillment of Isaiah's prophecy and the symbolism of light overcoming darkness. How do you see the light of Christ dispelling darkness in the world and in your personal life?

THE FOURTH LUMINOUS MYSTERY
The Transfiguration of Jesus

Now about eight days after these sayings Jesus took with him Peter and John and James, and went up on the mountain to pray. And while he was praying, the appearance of his face changed, and his clothes became dazzling white. Suddenly they saw two men, Moses and Elijah, talking to him. They appeared in glory and were speaking of his departure, which he was about to accomplish at Jerusalem. Now Peter and his companions were weighed down with sleep; but since they had stayed awake, they saw his glory and the two men who stood with him. Just as they were leaving him, Peter said to Jesus, 'Master, it is good for us to be here; let us make three dwellings, one for you, one for Moses, and one for Elijah'—not knowing what he said. While he was saying this, a cloud came and overshadowed them; and they were terrified as they entered the cloud. Then from the cloud came a voice that said, 'This is my Son, my Chosen; listen to him!' When the voice had spoken, Jesus was found alone. And they kept silent and in those days told no one any of these things they had seen.
Luke 9:28–36

Reflection Questions

1. Envision being on the mountain with Peter, John, and James on the mountain as they are witnesses to the Transfiguration. Imagine the landscape around

you, the feel of the sun, the wind. How does seeing Jesus in his glory affect your understanding of his divine nature?

2. Reflect on the voice from the cloud saying, "This is my Son, my Chosen; listen to him!" How can you better listen to and follow Jesus in your daily life?

THE FIFTH LUMINOUS MYSTERY
The Last Supper

Then came the day of Unleavened Bread, on which the Passover lamb had to be sacrificed. So Jesus sent Peter and John, saying, 'Go and prepare the Passover meal for us that we may eat it. . . .' When the hour came, he took his place at the table, and the apostles with him. He said to them, 'I have eagerly desired to eat this Passover with you before I suffer; for I tell you, I will not eat it until it is fulfilled in the kingdom of God. . . .' Then he took a loaf of bread, and when he had given thanks, he broke it and gave it to them, saying, 'This is my body, which is given for you. Do this in remembrance of me.' And he did the same with the cup after supper, saying, 'This cup that is poured out for you is the new covenant in my blood.' Luke 22:7–8, 14–16, 19–20

Reflection Questions

1. Imagine being present at the Last Supper, hearing Jesus speak about his body and blood. Look around you. Who else is there? How are they dressed? What is Peter doing? What about Judas? How do Jesus's words deepen your understanding of the Eucharist and its significance in your life?

2. Reflect on Jesus's desire to share this Passover meal with his disciples before his suffering. How does this demonstrate his love and commitment to them and to us?

THE
SORROWFUL MYSTERIES

THE FIRST SORROWFUL MYSTERY
The Agony in the Garden

Then Jesus went with them to a place called Gethsemane; and he said to his disciples, 'Sit here while I go over there and pray.' He took with him Peter and the two sons of Zebedee, and began to be grieved and agitated. Then he said to them, 'I am deeply grieved, even to death; remain here, and stay awake with me.' And going a little farther, he threw himself on the ground and prayed, 'My Father, if it is possible, let this cup pass from me; yet not what I want but what you want.' Then he came to the disciples and found them sleeping; and he said to Peter, 'So, could you not stay awake with me one hour?' Matthew 26:36–40

Reflection Questions

1. Picture yourself in the garden with Jesus as he prays. What does the garden look like? What fragrances are carried by the breeze? Could this be Eden at night? Does Jesus cry softly into his hands? Or is he sobbing? Does he seem hurt, or frightened, or angry? How do his words and emotions affect your understanding of his humanity and his sacrifice?

2. Reflect on Jesus's prayer, "Not what I want but what you want." How can you apply this attitude of surrender and trust to your own life, especially in difficult times?

THE SECOND SORROWFUL MYSTERY
The Scourging of Jesus at the Pillar

> Pilate spoke to them again, 'Then what do you wish me
> to do with the man you call the King of the Jews?' They
> shouted back, 'Crucify him!' Pilate asked them, 'Why,
> what evil has he done?' But they shouted all the more,
> 'Crucify him!' So Pilate, wishing to satisfy the crowd,
> released Barabbas for them; and after flogging Jesus, he
> handed him over to be crucified. Mark 15:12–15

Reflection Questions

1. Imagine witnessing the flogging of Jesus. Look
   around you and see the Roman soldiers and
   onlookers. What are they doing? What are the
   expressions on their faces? Does seeing his suffering
   affect your understanding of the price he paid for
   our sins?
2. Reflect on Pilate's decision to appease the crowd
   rather than seek justice. How can you stand firm in
   your convictions and faith, even, or especially, when
   faced with opposition or pressure?

THE THIRD SORROWFUL MYSTERY
The Crowning of Jesus with Thorns

Then the soldiers led him into the courtyard of the palace (that is, the governor's headquarters); and they called together the whole cohort. And they clothed him in a purple cloak; and after twisting some thorns into a crown, they put it on him. And they began saluting him, 'Hail, King of the Jews!' They struck his head with a reed, spat upon him, and knelt down in homage to him. After mocking him, they stripped him of the purple cloak and put his own clothes on him. Then they led him out to crucify him. Mark 15:16–20

Reflection Questions

1. Picture Jesus mocked and crowned with thorns. What does his face look like? What are the expressions of the soldiers? Pay attention to the sharpness of the thorns, the color of blood on sand. Would you trade places? Would you do this for him? Would you do it for your child? How does this scene deepen your understanding of Jesus's humility and love for humanity?

2. Reflect on the actions of the soldiers. Imagine what it would feel like to be the brunt of their mockery. How do you respond with love and dignity when faced with derision, mistreatment, or brutality in your own life?

THE FOURTH SORROWFUL MYSTERY
The Carrying of the Cross by Jesus

And carrying the cross by himself, he went out to what is called The Place of the Skull, which in Hebrew is called Golgotha. . . . As they led him away, they seized a man, Simon of Cyrene, who was coming from the country, and they laid the cross on him, and made him carry it behind Jesus. A great number of the people followed him, and among them were women who were beating their breasts and wailing for him. But Jesus turned to them and said, 'Daughters of Jerusalem, do not weep for me, but weep for yourselves and for your children.' John 19:17, Luke 23:26–28

Reflection Questions

1. Imagine walking alongside Jesus as he carries his cross. Picture his pain and suffering. What does he look like as he carries such a heavy weight? Where are his friends? Are they hidden away somewhere out of sight, or are they in the crowd? Are they weeping? Are they angry? Would you choose to be there if you could? Why? If you had the power to change anything, what would that one thing be?

How does witnessing the suffering and perseverance of Jesus impact your faith? Your understanding of his deep and penetrating love for you?

2. Reflect on Jesus's words to the women of Jerusalem. Do these words encourage you to focus on your own spiritual journey and on the well-being of those around you?

THE FIFTH SORROWFUL MYSTERY
The Crucifixion of Jesus

And carrying the cross himself, he went out to what is called The Place of the Skull, which in Hebrew is called Golgotha. There they crucified him, and with him two others, one on either side, with Jesus between them. . . . Meanwhile, standing near the cross of Jesus were his mother, and his mother's sister, Mary the wife of Clopas, and Mary Magdalene. When Jesus saw his mother and the disciple whom he loved standing beside her, he said to his mother, 'Woman, here is your son.' Then he said to the disciple, 'Here is your mother.' And from that hour the disciple took her to his own home. . . . It was now about noon, and darkness came over the whole land until three in the afternoon, while the sun's light failed; and the curtain of the temple was torn in two. Then Jesus, crying with a loud voice, said, 'Father, into your hands I commend my spirit.' Having said this, he breathed his last. John 19:17–18, 25–27; Luke 23:44–46

Reflection Questions

1. Picture yourself at the foot of the cross. First, imagine yourself as a bystander: What do you see? What are you doing? Then cast yourself as a Roman soldier: What do you experience as you watch this man die? Do you feel guilty? Complicit? Regretful?

Finally, reflect upon how being present at the moment of Jesus's crucifixion expands your understanding of his sacrifice and love.

2. Reflect on Jesus's words, "Father, into your hands I commend my spirit." How can you emulate Jesus's trust in God? How might your own surrender to God take expression?

THE
GLORIOUS MYSTERIES

THE FIRST GLORIOUS MYSTERY
The Resurrection

But the angel said to the women, 'Do not be afraid; I know that you are looking for Jesus who was crucified. He is not here; for he has been raised, as he said. Come, see the place where he lay. Then go quickly and tell his disciples, "He has been raised from the dead, and indeed he is going ahead of you to Galilee; there you will see him." This is my message for you.' So they left the tomb quickly with fear and great joy, and ran to tell his disciples. Suddenly Jesus met them and said, 'Greetings!' And they came to him, took hold of his feet, and worshiped him. Then Jesus said to them, 'Do not be afraid; go and tell my brothers to go to Galilee; there they will see me.' Matthew 28:5–10

Reflection Questions

1. Imagine being one of the women at the tomb, hearing the angel's message, and encountering the risen Jesus. How does this encounter with the risen Christ inspire hope and joy in your life?

2. Reflect on Jesus's command to the women to "go and tell." In your daily life, how might you share the message of the Resurrection with others?

THE SECOND GLORIOUS MYSTERY
The Ascension of Jesus to Heaven

So when they had come together, they asked him, 'Lord, is this the time when you will restore the kingdom to Israel?' He replied, 'It is not for you to know the times or periods that the Father has set by his own authority. But you will receive power when the Holy Spirit has come upon you; and you will be my witnesses in Jerusalem, in all Judea and Samaria, and to the ends of the earth.' When he had said this, as they were watching, he was lifted up, and a cloud took him out of their sight. Acts 1:6–9

Reflection Questions

1. Picture yourself among the disciples as Jesus ascends into heaven. What does this event actually look like? How are Jesus's family and friends responding? Is there a collective gasp in the crowd? Do they try to talk Jesus out of leaving them? How does witnessing the Ascension strengthen your faith and understanding of Jesus's divine mission?

2. Reflect on Jesus's promise to send the Holy Spirit to his disciples and the call to be his witnesses. How can you be a witness to Christ in your community and beyond?

THE THIRD GLORIOUS MYSTERY
The Descent of the Holy Spirit upon the Apostles

When the day of Pentecost had come, they were all together in one place. And suddenly from heaven there came a sound like the rush of a violent wind, and it filled the entire house where they were sitting. Divided tongues, as of fire, appeared among them, and a tongue rested on each of them. All of them were filled with the Holy Spirit and began to speak in other languages, as the Spirit gave them ability. Acts 2:1–4

Reflection Questions

1. Imagine being in the room with the disciples when the Holy Spirit descends. Imagine the mighty wind that fills the room. What do the tongues of fire look like? Do you feel the heat? Does the fire singe the air? What has happened to the disciples around you? Have they changed? What is it that they say in these different tongues? How does the presence of the Holy Spirit inspire and empower you in your faith journey?

2. Reflect on how the disciples were transformed after receiving the Holy Spirit. How can you allow the Holy Spirit to guide and strengthen you in your daily life and actions?

THE FOURTH GLORIOUS MYSTERY
The Assumption of Mary

A great portent appeared in heaven: a woman clothed with the sun, with the moon under her feet, and on her head a crown of twelve stars. Revelation 12:1

Reflection Questions

1. Visualize the image of Mary clothed with the sun and crowned with stars. How bright are the stars that crown her head? Are the stars themselves alive with emotion? Do they enjoy this moment so close to Mary? Does Mary wear them well, or is she too humble to carry them proudly? What sounds do you hear? What are Mary's last words to her friends? How does this vision of Mary's assumption inspire your devotion to her and extend your understanding of her role in salvation history?

2. Ponder the significance of Mary being taken up into heaven. How does her assumption give you hope for your own eternal destiny with God?

THE FIFTH GLORIOUS MYSTERY
The Crowning of Mary as the Queen of Heaven

I will greatly rejoice in the LORD, my whole being shall exult in my God; for he has clothed me with the garments of salvation, he has covered me with the robe of righteousness, as a bridegroom decks himself with a garland, and as a bride adorns herself with her jewels. Isaiah 61:10

Reflection Questions

1. Picture Mary being crowned as Queen of Heaven. Imagine the crown. What could it possibly be made of? Grace? Can grace attain a form? Then again, is there anything that could improve or elevate the beauty of Mary? Why should she wear any crown other than something too glorious for us to even imagine here on earth? Is anyone standing nearby? What do you see? What do you feel? How does Mary's coronation reflect God's glory and the honor given to her as the mother of Jesus?

2. Reflect on the joy and exultation described in Isaiah's prophecy. How can you cultivate a spirit of joy and gratitude in your relationship with God and in your daily life?

AFTERWORD

PRAYER AND HEALING FROM TRAUMA

As I put the finishing touches on this book, I feel compelled to add a few words about how prayer and, more specifically, the Rosary in particular, can help people who are suffering from trauma of any kind. Trauma, as I have come to understand, leaves an imprint not only on our minds but also on our hearts and in our bodies. When trauma fractures the soul, prayer is a process that can restore the broken bits. I consider these thoughts a preamble to my forthcoming book with the working title *Be Still*. This book explores the cultivation of stillness in our lives, and the benefits we gain from doing so.

When we experience trauma, the effects linger long after the event has passed. Our bodies remember, often in ways we are not fully aware of. Trauma creates a sense of disconnection—from ourselves, from others, and from the world around us. Healing begins when we find a way to feel safe again, both physically and emotionally.

This is where the power of prayer, and particularly praying the Rosary, can be profoundly helpful in the healing process.

Trauma distorts how we see ourselves and the world. Trauma can fill us with shame, guilt, or unworthiness. But in prayer, we are given an entry point to a deeper truth: we are no less than God's own beloved children, and through God's grace, we can shed a false sense of who we are.

It is no accident that the mysteries of the Rosary reflect the full spectrum of human experience. They remind us that, like Christ, even though we are called to carry our crosses, healing and the safe place of hope and resurrection await.

Prayer, when practiced with intentionality, can help to gently release stored trauma; it is a way of entering into sacred space, where we can find the grace to not only survive the memory of things that have happened to us, but to be renewed by those occasions.

Prayer leads us on a path toward healing—one that helps us reconnect with ourselves, with God, and with the deeper truths that trauma often obscures. It is my hope that the reflections in this book offer comfort to those who are hurting, and a sense of peace for those who seek healing. As I conclude this book, I can give you no greater gift than to invite you to journey into the wide, wondrous stillness where God's healing grace resides.

ACKNOWLEDGMENTS

I am deeply grateful to the wonderful people at Loyola Press, including Joellyn Ciccarelli, Santiago Cortes, John Christensen, Kim Skalman, Donna Antkowiak, Cepheus Edmondson, Jill Arena, Madeline Ramirez, Rob Ferry, Carrie Freyer, Andrew Yankech, and Mary Alice Howard, for their invaluable support.

A heartfelt thank you to my copyeditor, Crane Giamo, and proofreaders Susan Taylor and Alison Shurtz for the fantastic job of sanding and polishing this manuscript.

To Maura Poston, my editor, your care and goodwill in revising and refining this manuscript have improved everything about it. Maura, you are an invaluable editor, but more important, you are a dear friend who has stood by me for nearly twenty years. Your guidance, support, and unwavering loyalty have been a cornerstone in my life. Thank you, Maura, for everything.

Finally, I want to offer my thanks and love to my wife, Grace, and my sons, Edward and Charles. I am proud of the beautiful, kind, intelligent, and fascinating people you are, and I love you all to the moon and back. Your love and support are my foundation, and I am grateful for each of you every day.

FURTHER READING

BOOKS ON THE ROSARY

Groeschel, Benedict J. *The Rosary: Chain of Hope.* San Francisco, CA: Ignatius Press, 2003.

Guardini, Romano. *The Rosary of Our Lady.* Nashus, NH: Sophia Institute Press, 1998.

Sri, Edward. *Praying the Rosary Like Never Before.* Ann Arbor, MI: Servant Books, 2017.

Longenecker, Dwight. *Praying the Rosary for Spiritual Warfare.* Irondale, AL: EWTN Publishing, 2016.

Marcellino, Kathryn. *Scriptural Rosary: How to Pray the Rosary and Meditate on the Mysteries.* Modesto, CA: Abundant Life Publishing, 2018.

Montfort, St. Louis de. *The Secret of the Rosary.* Gastonia, NC: TAN Books, 1993.

BOOKS ON WELLNESS AND HEALTH

Bourne, Edmund J. *The Anxiety and Phobia Workbook.* Oakland, CA: New Harbinger Publications, 2020.

Chopra, Deepak, and Rudolph E. Tanzi. *Super Brain: Unleashing the Explosive Power of Your Mind to Maximize Health, Happiness, and Spiritual Well-Being*. Lagos, Nigeria: Harmony, 2012.

Chopra, Deepak, and Rudolph E. Tanzi. *The Healing Self: A Revolutionary New Plan to Supercharge Your Immunity and Stay Well for Life*. Lagos, Nigeria: Harmony, 2018.

Kolk, Bessel van der. *The Body Keeps the Score: Brain, Mind, and Body in the Healing of Trauma*. New York: Penguin Books, 2014.

Perlmutter, David. *Grain Brain: The Surprising Truth About Wheat, Carbs, and Sugar—Your Brain's Silent Killers*. rev. ed. Little, New York: Little, Brown Spark, 2018.

Siegel, Bernie S. *The Art of Healing: Uncovering Your Inner Wisdom and Potential for Self-Healing*. Novato, CA: New World Library, 2013.

NOTES

Epigraph.   Catechism of the Catholic Church
(Washington, DC, United States Conference
of Catholic Bishops, 2006, 2007), no. 2798.
Dedication. Jack Kerouac, *The Sea is My Brother*
(Cambridge, MA: Da Capo Press, 2011).

1.   Gary Jansen, *Holy Ghosts: Or, How a (Not-So) Good
Catholic Boy Became a Believer in Things That Go Bump
in the Night* (New York: Jeremy P. Tarcher/Penguin,
2010).
Gary Jansen, *Station to Station: An Ignatian Journey
through the Stations of the Cross* (Chicago: Loyola Press,
2017).

2.   Sister Thérèse of Lisieux, *Story of a Soul: The
Autobiography of the Little Flower, St. Therese of Lisieux*
(TAN Books, 2010).

3.   Benedict XVI, pastoral visit to Palermo, October 3,
2010, https://www.vatican.va/content/benedict-xvi/
en/speeches/2010/october/documents/hf_ben-xvi_
spe_20101003_palermo-giovani.html.

4. *Rosarium Virginis Mariae* by John Paul II, The Holy See, 2002. https://www.vatican.va/content/john-paul-ii/en/apost_letters/2002/documents/hf_jp-ii_apl_20021016_rosarium-virginis-mariae.html

5. Romano Guardini, *The Rosary of Our Lady* (Nashua, NH: Sophia Institute Press, 1998).

6. Rainer Maria Rilke, *Letters to a Young Poet*, trans. by M. D. Herter Norton (New York: W. W. Norton & Company, Inc., 1962), 27.

7. Gary Jansen, *MicroShifts: Transforming Your Life One Step at a Time* (Chicago: Loyola Press, 2019)

8. Bessel van der Kolk, in *The Body Keeps the Score*, as quoted by Maria Shriver, https://mariashriver.com/breaking-the-silence/.

9, Antoine de Saint-Exupéry, *The Little Prince* (San Diego: Harcourt Brace & Company, 1971), 75.

10. van der Kolk, *The Body Keeps the Score*, page 127.

11. https://www.mayoclinic.org/tests-procedures/meditation/in-depth/meditation/art-20045858

12. https://pmc.ncbi.nlm.nih.gov/articles/PMC7917055/

13. https://pmc.ncbi.nlm.nih.gov/articles/PMC5859128/

ABOUT THE AUTHOR

Gary Jansen is the author of several bestselling books, including the memoir *Holy Ghosts: Or, How a (Not So) Good Catholic Boy Became a Believer in Things That Go Bump in the Night*, and *The 15-Minute Prayer Solution*, *Station to Station*, and the multi-award winning *MicroShifts: Transforming Your Life One Step at a Time*. His illustrated children's book, *Remember Us with Smiles*, which he co-wrote with his wife Grace Jansen, won the 2023 Christopher Award in the Books for Young People category.

Jansen's work has received high praise from prominent figures, including international bestselling author Paulo Coelho, who called his writing "Wonderful," and legendary *Newsweek* editor Kenneth L. Woodward, in whose opinion Jansen is "A fine writer." Jansen, a frequent speaker, has been featured on NPR, The Huffington Post, CNN.com, Coast to Coast AM, A&E, the Sundance Channel, and has appeared numerous times on the Travel Channel's *Mysteries at the Museum and Beyond the Unknown*.

**Winner of the Christopher Award
for Books for Young Readers**

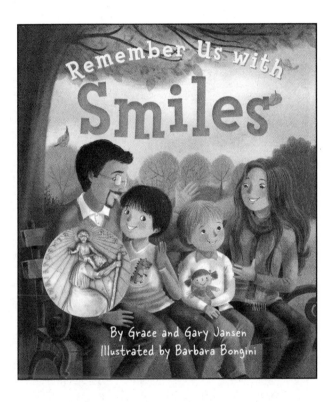

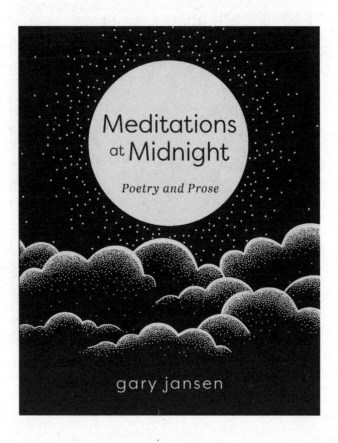

Meditations
at Midnight

Poetry and Prose

gary jansen